Learning Mathematics Successfully

Raising Self-Efficacy in Students, Teachers, and Parents

Learning Mathematics Successfully

Raising Self-Efficacy in Students, Teachers, and Parents

By

Clark J. Hickman and Helene J. Sherman
University of Missouri-St. Louis

Information Age Publishing, Inc.
Charlotte, North Carolina • www.infoagepub.com

Library of Congress Cataloging-in-Publication Data

CIP data for this book can be found on the Library of Congress website:
http://www.loc.gov/index.html

Paperback: 978-1-64113-737-9
Hardcover: 978-1-64113-738-6
E-Book: 978-1-64113-739-3

CONTENTS

ACKNOWLEDGMENTS

Writing a book about innovative teaching practices cannot be done in isolation. We are immensely grateful to our students who have inspired us to hone our theories and practices through insightful questions and realistic feedback. Today's teacher education candidates are among the brightest and enthusiastic beginning teachers we have seen. It is through their eyes and experiences that we gained insight into the development of a teacher from novice to seasoned. We also thank our colleagues at the University of Missouri-St. Louis who consistently offered encouragement, support, as well as guidance and sage advice.

We owe a debt of gratitude to Lisa Brown, Frank Aguirre, and Yulia Brook of Information Age Publishing and to Natalie Morrison, Joan Barnidge, and David Kopp for their constructive feedback on the content and design of this book. Their feedback strengthened our work and helped make complex ideas clear.

Finally, we thank our families, especially Carl Sherman, Gwen Hickman, and Robert Wright, for their never-ending support of our absenteeism during the researching and writing of this book. Their encouragement to continue our writing during many long months is very much appreciated.

Clark J. Hickman
Helene J. Sherman

CHAPTER 1

FOUNDATIONS OF SOCIAL LEARNING THEORY AND SELF-EFFICACY

Teaching, Learning, and Mentoring

HOW WE LEARN

The Learning Triad

Today's mathematics students are part of a reciprocal triad consisting of themselves, their parents or guardian, and their teacher. Each component influences student learning. As students progress through their academic coursework, they are influenced and sensitive to overt—and subtle—feedback from these primary sources, as well as by internal feedback, which often mirrors the feedback of significant adults. Lastly, they are influenced, consciously and unconsciously, by their peers. Comparisons are made as to how successful they are, relative to their classmates. Am I catching on to this? Do I understand it? Can I answer a test question? Why is it so "easy" for some? Why can't others keep up? Students are bombarded with a myriad of feedback cues throughout the day, trying to determine if they measure up to their teacher's and family's expectations, and how they are doing relative to their peers.

Learning Mathematics Successfully: Raising Self-Efficacy in Students, Teachers, and Parents
pp. 1–22
Copyright © 2019 by Information Age Publishing

Teachers, as one component of the triad, are seeking feedback cues as well. They may ask themselves, "Do my students understand this?" "How can I explain this math concept succinctly?" "How well do I, myself, understand the mathematical unit, and the theories that underlie it?" "Do the parents understand what I am trying to accomplish in this course, and are they supportive of both the curriculum and their child?" "Do my colleagues understand and support my teaching style, and do I get feedback from them that my students are prepared to go to the next level once they leave my class?" Lastly, as teachers, they are influenced by professional development requirements of their school, and keep an eye on legislated mandates requiring new standards and curriculum, they may question whether or not they can keep up with the changes and requirements or even if they believe in them.

The third part of the triad is the family. Adults are not in the classroom as either teacher or student. But, they usually represent a critical component of the student's feedback system and directly affect a student's feeling of self-worth and confidence. Caretakers certainly want the best for their child, including the best teachers, curriculum, and environments in which to learn and thrive. Parents look for feedback too, such as how their student is doing. Are they struggling? Do they understand (and respect) the teacher? Do I understand what the teacher is trying to do in the unit or class? How can I help my student? *Can* I help my student—do I even understand the material and how it is now being taught? When should I help? How much should I help? How can I be encouraging?

Triad Influences on Students, Teachers and Family: Learning

Let us look at this triad in operation. Bob is 12 years old and a student in middle school math. He earns average grades and does not fear math, though it is not his favorite subject, either. Up to now, he has earned mostly Bs and Cs on tests, with the occasional A if he "lucked out" as he says, or even a few Ds if he "forgot to study." He has been told by his family that he needs a grounding in math to succeed in life, and believes that at face value, even though he does not understand exactly what kind of math, or what that even means. As the coursework gets more complicated with every year, he is starting to feel intimidated by the prospect of tackling Algebra I and Algebra II in high school, let alone geometry and maybe calculus. He wants to do well, he wants to go to college, and he wants to have a good career that pays well, even though he does not know what that is going to be yet. Most of all, at this point, he wants his family to feel proud and not let them down. He also does not want to fail and have to repeat a course, lest he have to "suffer through that stuff again" or be embarrassed in front of his classmates. His parents tell him "you can do it," but can he? What if he can't? What evidence does he have that he can really do well in math? He is looking for feedback.

Ms. Johnson is Bob's teacher. She has been teaching middle school math for 10 years. She always knew she wanted to be a teacher and got high grades in the math and sciences in high school. Ms. Johnson loved these subjects and wanted to convey her enthusiasm to the next generation of students. She knew that she could teach in a way that students would not only learn, but that her love and passion for mathematics would be contagious. When she began teaching, she developed her style and curriculum with gusto. As semesters turned into years, she realized that not all students shared her passion and enthusiasm for math. In fact, a sizeable number were just getting through it. Families seemed either intimidated, critical, or withdrawn from their student's work. She was pressed by district, state, and national mandates to change her curriculum and how it was taught: Now what mattered was how her students scored on mandated standardized tests and it was *these* results that mattered to her supervisors. Ms. Johnson eventually went from looking forward to each incoming class as a challenge and opportunity, to looking forward to school breaks. This teacher needs feedback too: Is she succeeding in teaching the content? Is she keeping up with the latest methodology, let alone latest mandates on what must be taught? How can she regain her enthusiasm for teaching and passion for her subject? How can she develop a more productive relationship with parents? Is this the right career for her now? Can she do this?

Bob's parents are Laura and Mike. They both work outside the home building their own careers, but at least one of them tries to attend PTA meetings and parent-teacher conferences if possible. They glance over communication from the school about Bob's schedule and coursework, and the expectations the teachers have for him, and try to be supportive and reinforcing on what the teachers are trying to teach. Neither Laura nor Mike majored in math, and do not use it as a focus of their jobs. Yet, they feel, as many do, that a grounding in math is important to get into college and have a successful career. Knowing that some children get frustrated and do not do well in math, Laura and Mike keep an eye on his grades and try to sense whether he is happy with the subject, happy with his teacher, or is feeling frustrated and like a failure. They also realize that it has been 35 years since either one of them were in middle school math themselves, so they are curious as to what Bob is learning—and how it is being taught. While they are largely satisfied with Bob's progress and grades, they also remember a few instances in which Bob expressed fits of frustration—even tears—at not being able to figure out a problem. They also remember not being sure how to help, and would explaining it "their way" be so different from the current teaching method, that it actually confused Bob instead of helping him? Lastly, they wonder how much "pressure" to exert on Bob. Certainly, they do not want to put on so much pressure to do well that he becomes incapacitated with anxiety; but, on the other hand, they do not want him to become complacent to the point where "just getting by" is good enough. They may be asking themselves: How do we try to be supportive and reinforcing without saying "good job!" when it is really only mediocre? How do we maintain interest and connection, without hovering and being annoying? What does the teacher want us to do? What are other parents doing? How do we not misstep here?

Bob, his teacher Ms. Johnson, and his parents, Mike and Laura represent people and scenarios playing out all across the country on a daily basis. Their issues are not uncommon, yet failing to address each member of the triad's need for appropriate feedback and examples of success can impede Bob's ability to feel he can succeed in learning math. While Bob, his teacher, and parents all want Bob to succeed, the teacher and parents also want to succeed in their respective roles as well. Each is faced with assessing their own level of competence, and their beliefs in whether or not they can succeed as a student, teacher, or parent.

SOCIAL LEARNING THEORIES

An approach to lifelong learning—whether it be by students, their families or teachers—can be framed by social learning and self-efficacy theories. Albert Bandura (1986) is a social learning theorist who explains human behavior in terms of three components:

- personal/cognitive understanding;
- behavior; and
- environment.

Personal/cognitive components refer to the thinking process—examples include one's perceptions and judgments about one's ability to perform an assignment; one's perceptions of internal strengths and weaknesses; and one's thoughts about rewards (or lack thereof) of doing a task successfully. Behavior components refer to beliefs about the act of actually performing a behavior—for example, completing a homework assignment. Students might be asking themselves if they know the steps to find a solution. Environmental components refer to those variables outside of the individual that would either help or hinder, successful completion of the task. Examples could include available time, a safe work area,

adequate sleep and nutrition, and perceived attitudes of significant people in the student's sphere: usually, family members, teachers, and
friends/peers (i.e., do they care, and does it matter to them if I'm successful?).

Defining Social Learning Theory

Social learning theory explains human behavior in terms of "reciprocal
determinism," which implies a "reciprocal interaction between cognitive,
behavioral, and environmental determinants" (Bandura, 1977b, p. 204).
Previous views considered behavior a function and interaction of the person and the environment. Reciprocal determinism emphasizes the roles
of behavior, the person, and the environment on subsequent behavior. In
other words, a person is more than just thoughts, just behaviors, or simply
products of their environments. People's motivation to learn, and complete a project is a psychological assessment involving their own thoughts
regarding their beliefs, as confirmed through their behaviors and environment. People are therefore neither "victims" of the environment, nor
are they totally free agents to become whatever they choose (Bandura,
1986). Thoughts influence behavior, behavior then reinforces (or
changes) thoughts, and the reaction of the environment to both the
behavior and thoughts (or attitude) further refines both the thoughts and
behavior.

Bandura's model of social learning theory appears as a triad of reciprocal influences between personal/cognitive factors, the environment, and
behavior with each factor influencing the other (Bandura, 1986).

"Personal/Cognitive" Influences: This element refers to an individual's
conceptions, beliefs, self-perceptions, intentions, and preferences (Bandura, 1986). Using our example above, the "personal/cognitive" refers to
Bob and his attitudes toward learning math. How does he perceive math
(easy, moderately hard, difficult, or impossible)? How does he internally
judge his ability to learn new math concepts? How does he prefer to
tackle new assignments? What are his overall perceptions of his abilities in
learning math? Finally, what are his beliefs about the value of doing so?

Behavior Influences: This element of the model refers to actions of the
individual that occur in reciprocal relation to thought processes and environmental influences (Bandura, 1986). That is, the environmental cues
Bob receives, blended with his internal thought processes, are going to be
major determinants of his *behavior*—what he is willing to actually *do?* If
Bob has perceptions about himself and his ability that are positive, coupled with a supportive and encouraging environment, chances are that
his behavior (actively engaging in learning math, persisting in difficulties,

and studying hard to ensure success) will reflect his positive disposition and his positive environment. Conversely, if he is discouraged, has a poor image of himself and/or his mathematical abilities, and has a nonencouraging environment, the chances that he is going to engage in the types of behaviors necessary for success in math are greatly diminished.

Environmental Influences: These can modify thoughts and feelings through observed modeling, instruction, or social persuasion (Bandura, 1986). Bob, in our example, is not learning math in isolation. He is surrounded by conscious and unconscious stimuli throughout his math periods, and into the evening doing homework at home. How competent does he judge his teacher? How "friendly" or approachable does he perceive that teacher if he gets stuck? What is his perception of the expectations his parents have on him to do well? How are his fellow students doing—does he think he's keeping up, or are other students "getting it" faster than him? What sort of messages is he hearing from the outside world as to the value (or not) of understanding math?

This behavioral model of personal conceptions, environmental influences, and behavior is not only confined to the student, in our case, Bob. Bob's teacher, Ms. Johnson, is also operating in a similar model herself, as are his parents, Mike and Laura. For Ms. Johnson, she needs to be aware of her competence in not only understanding mathematical principles herself, but how to teach them so students understand them. Initially, she received this feedback from her math teachers and then university professors and supervisors. Now, she receives feedback by environmental cues such as student interest, the types of questions they ask, how well they do on exams, and comments she gets from parents. The personal perceptions and environmental feedback she receives—whether it be something as blunt as a direct conversation with a colleague, parent, or student, or something much more subtle such as student yawning or glazed eyes—all factor together into her behaviors: How much effort is she going to expend thinking about new and effective ways to impart this content? How much effort is she going to expend probing possible problems and areas of confusion? How much professional development is she going to seek out to grow as a teacher? The extent to which Ms. Johnson is *aware* of the information she is processing, and its source, is the extent to which she can seek out solutions to whatever weaknesses in her teaching she perceives. Is she feeling insecure about her understanding of the material she is asked to teach? Is she feeling the students do not understand the value, and are thus bored or show little effort? What feedback does she need, and how can she get it?

Bob's parents, Laura and Mike, are almost certainly not consciously aware of this psychological model under which they are operating. But, from their perspective, their understanding of their own mathematical abilities specifically, and their general feelings of parental competence, coupled with environmental feedback, determines how they are going to react (their behavior) to Bob's progress. What feedback are they receiving from Bob? Complaints? Happiness and satisfaction? What's his level of motivation? What feedback are they getting from the teacher via conferences or report cards? Are they aware of how their own perceptions of their mathematical abilities may be consciously, or unconsciously, transferred to Bob? How do they match their reactions (behavior) to the information presented to them by Bob or his teacher? Do they put on more pressure, back off, or remain steady? How do they know what to do?

Self-Efficacy Theory

The foundational principles of self-efficacy theory are found between the two anchors of locus of control (Rotter, 1966) and Albert Bandura's social cognitive theory (1977a). The common element of these theories has been the emphasis on *human agency*—the idea that humans, themselves, exercise control over actions that affect their lives (Zee & Koomen, 2016; see also Bandura, 1986, 1997). Drawing on earlier works, Rotter conceptualized "locus of control" as a *generalized* set of expectations that individuals develop, based on experiences with their environments, usually in the form of reinforcements. Rotter assumed that people differed in their perceptions of whether outcomes were the result of luck, fate, or the kindness/evil of other people (referred to as *external),* or the result of their own actions, such as hard work, dedication, discipline—or lack thereof (referred to as *internal).* Thus, those who had adopted an external locus of control had perceived themselves as either being a beneficiary of a friendly environment. For example, some might consider that luck was the main contributor to getting an A because the test was easy or that they got the promotion because the boss liked them. Likewise, people could think they are a victim of a nasty and unfair environment if they failed because the teacher asked all the wrong questions or wasn't promoted because the boss didn't like them or that their students failed themselves. In short, with an external orientation, everything good that happens to me is luck or good fate; anything bad that happens to me is me living under a nasty cloud—in neither case do I attribute my success or failure to anything *I* did.

Contrasting that with an internal locus of control perception, a person will credit a good grade or promotion with competence, hard work, study, and being worthy of the reward; they will credit poor grades and missed promotions as lack of preparation, or failing to meet expectations. According to Rotter, those who tend to attribute successes and failures to their own actions tend to be more self-motivated, happier, can more easily adapt to change, can more easily overcome obstacles, and be more successful as a student, teacher, or employee (Rotter, 1966).

Using Rotter as a theoretical foundation, the Rand Corporation incorporated two brief items on a lengthy 1976 survey of California teachers that attempted to assess teachers' attitudes about whether they, as teachers, could positively affect student learning (Armor et al., 1976, p. 73):

- "When it comes right down to it, a teacher really can't do much because most of a student's motivation and performance depends on his or her home environment."
- "If I really try hard, I can get through to even the most difficult or unmotivated students."

These two items formed the basis for initial scholarly investigations into the complex psychological systems operating in a classroom between students and teachers, and even within the students' and teachers' own minds. Zee and Kooman (2016) point out the most prominent of these as the teacher's locus of control study (Rose & Medway, 1981), Guskey's (1981) responsibility for student achievement, and the Webb Efficacy Scale (Ashton, Olejnik, Crocker, & McAuliffe, 1982). (Chapter 4 examines, in more detail, the assessment of self-efficacy levels, and the basis on which modern assessment instruments are formed.)

Building on Rotter's theory, Albert Bandura argued that people are not only motivated by generalized expectancies, as Rotter had claimed, but that people were also influenced by what they perceived as their capabilities—their *self-efficacy*—in judging whether or not to perform actions in particular areas. To further emphasize his point, Bandura (1977a) made clear a distinction between response-outcome expectancies and self-efficacy expectations. In other words, response-outcome expectations refer to individuals' estimates "that a given behavior will lead to certain outcomes" (Bandura, 1977b, p. 193).

With self-efficacy theory, though, Bandura (1977a) argues that a teacher or student may *know* that a given action or behavior may lead to a positive outcome, but feel this information is useless if they believe they lack the abilities to produce behaviors leading to the those outcomes. One will not attempt a behavior (e.g., a new teaching method) that one does not feel capable of performing successfully. Bandura asserts that it is personal self-efficacy that is the primary cause of human behavior (Bandura, 1977a).

Recall that self-efficacy theory is a component of social learning theory. For example, let's say a teacher wants to begin a unit on dividing fractions. The teacher can do all sorts of things to convince students that they can successfully divide fractions—they can tell them, show them, and guide them through the operation. They can even have students demonstrate their mastery. However, doing this—while important—is only one half of the teacher's task. The other half is the teacher articulating the outcomes the students desire in mastering the content. Such outcomes could be good grades on a test (or, not receiving a failing grade), the ability to move to another topic, and how it serves as a foundation for advanced topics. It is these desired outcomes that serve as an important motivator in the face of obstacles and frustration. If a student is struggling with mastering content, and cannot see the value of mastering it anyway, it is very easy to give up. When a student sighs in frustration and says, "What is the value of this anyway?" what he or she is really saving is "I don't understand the value of learning this." A student's sense of efficacy will be an equally critical factor in explaining how much effort they expend in the face of obstacles and learning difficulties. That is, for a person to try a new behavior (e.g. learn a new math operation), two elements must be present: First, the person must believe that they can learn and successfully perform the operation—even if it is eventually through trial and error—and, second, that successfully performing will lead to a desired outcome. Thus, self-efficacy is a critical element in understanding the motivational factors of students, their families, and teachers in terms of persistence to succeed. As such, Bandura distinguishes between *"efficacy expectations"* (the belief that one can successfully perform a behavior) and *"outcome expectations"* (the belief that if a behavior is performed, it will lead to a desired outcome) as two distinct and primary (although not exclusive) determinants of behavior (Bandura, 1977a, p. 79, 1977b, 1982a, 1982b, 1986).

It is Bandura's contention that levels of self-efficacy determine whether behavior change or coping strategies will be attempted or initiated, the amount of effort that will be expended, and the amount of time expended in the face of failures or other obstacles (Bandura, 1977b). This idea of efficacy and outcome expectations, of course, applies to both teachers as well as students. Regarding the relevance of social learning/self-efficacy theory to educational thinking, Ashton (1985) found that "a teachers' sense of efficacy ... is expected to influence the teachers' choice of instructional activities, the amount of effort they expend in teaching, and the degree of persistence they maintain when confronted with difficulties" (p. 144). Through assessing—even informally—levels of efficacy, and knowing how to elevate them, teachers can effectively raise that student's chances of success in mastering the content of a course. Specific strategies for assessing, then affecting, levels of self-efficacy will be thoroughly explored further in this book.

Sources of Self-Efficacy

There are four primary sources of self-efficacy in human behavior, which are discussed here in order of their strength of influence (Bandura, 1986). It is important to remember that these are not the only determinants of self-efficacy but, rather, the four primary influences. It is also important to remember that some of these sources vary in importance between individuals, and in context. In almost all cases, though, self-efficacy is influenced by these influences, in this order:

- enactive mastery,
- vicarious experiences,
- verbal persuasion, and
- physiological states.

Table 1.1 identifies these influences and common ways math teachers (and parents) can use them to heighten a student's level of self-efficacy.

Enactive Mastery

Sometimes referred to as "*enactive attainment,*" this source of self-efficacy is the most influential of all the sources. It refers to a person successfully engaging in a *specific* desired behavior to achieve a desired outcome. For example, many students believe that they can perform a mathematical operation on command *because they have done it* before successfully, and they understand the reasoning behind the exercise. Let's say our student, Bob, is learning how to add fractions. He understands the concept of adding fractions and can correctly compute combinations such as ¾ + ½. Bob practices with self-made practice examples and checks his work with a calculator. As a result, Bob feels confident he can add any set of fractions presented to him. At this point, Bob has attained mastery in adding fractions and his self-efficacy level is quite high. Recall, though, that self-efficacy refers to *specific* behaviors for *specific* tasks. While Bob's self-efficacy level for adding fractions is likely high after his successfully mastering the operation that does not mean that he *necessarily* has a high level of self-efficacy toward mathematics in general. Operations such as multiplication, division and subtraction are not the same as addition, and require a different (albeit related) skill set. Nevertheless, having heightened self-efficacy in one specific area, such as, addition of fractions, would likely enable Bob to approach tasks such as multiplication, division, and subtraction with more confidence than if he had failed and given up on addition.

Table 1.1.   Primary Influences of Self-Efficacy on Math Learners

Influences	Parent-Teacher Activity	Student Reaction Low SE	Student Reaction High SE	Goal
Enactive mastery	• Give students opportunity to successfully perform operation. Might require finding level of competence and build from there.	• "I can't" • "Why do I need to do this?" • "How is this important to me?" • Nonverbals of disapproval, boredom, or resistance.	• Attempts to perform operation. • Asks relevant clarifying questions.	• To successfully perform operation on command.
Vicarious experience	• Demonstrate how an operation is performed. Have qualified students perform the operations for each other.	• "I don't get it." • "I'm not as smart as them." • Nonverbals of distraction and inattentiveness.	• Wants to try to solve problems themselves.	• To successfully perform the operation themselves.
Verbal persuasion	• Words of encouragement to convince student that they have the ability to learn this math lesson and the reasons why it is important.	• "No, I can't." • "Yes, but …" • "I won't be able to get this." • "This is too hard for me." • Nonverbals of blank stares, frowns, rolled eyes.	• "Okay." • "Good, let's go." • "You're here to help, right?"	• To send positive and encouraging messages to students to give them courage to try.
Physiological states	• Look for cues that the students is physically upset or agitated. Stress level too high.	• Fidgety, sweaty palms, acts nervous.	• Calm, acting normally.	• Reduce stress overload that could interfere with learning.

Vicarious Experience

Whereas enactive mastery is the most powerful influence in attaining self-efficacy toward a behavior (e.g., performing a specific mathematical operation), it is not the sole influence. Watching others who are considered equal in ability successfully perform a task can also influence an individual's level of self-efficacy. We know that our perceptions of our ability to perform a task can be markedly influenced by watching, or visualizing, others perform the same task successfully (Bandura, 1986). In fact, even if we feel competent and confident in performing an operation, we are still influenced by the experiences of others with whom we share an identity as a peer. For instance, in our example above, Bob now feels confident in adding fractions. His classmate Tiffany, with whom he feels shares like-abilities, has also mastered adding fractions but understands it in slightly different ways and performs the operations somewhat differently—more efficiently or elegantly. Bob could be easily influenced to listen to her rationale and understand how a more efficient operation is actually faster and perhaps more accurate.

Vicarious experiences are also impactful in situations where external feedback is important in knowing whether or not one has mastered a behavior (e.g., adding fractions), and/or knowing whether peers are also mastering the content easily—or with difficulty. If Bob struggles with a mathematical operation, and he sees his classmates likewise struggling, this is important information for him to have to know that he is not alone in his confusion or frustration. Conversely, if Bob finds himself alone in his struggles—that his classmates easily understood the concepts but he did not—that, too, is valuable information for him so that he can investigate where the "disconnect" is occurring. In other words, "why are they getting it and not me?"

Unfortunately for the teacher and parents, Bob is unlikely to vocalize this very critical component of his self-efficacy. He is unlikely to tell either his teacher or his parents "everyone seems to be getting this except me— what am I doing wrong?" Instead, he is likely to wonder this to himself, or more damagingly, decide he is not as "good" as his classmate-peers and give up to save himself the frustration and embarrassment. This is why it is important for teachers to be aware of what struggling students are observing around them, and be able to intervene in effective ways. One way could be "verbal persuasion" discussed below. Another way could be to create opportunities for mastery discussed above. Subsequent parts of this book will provide additional practical strategies for teachers (and even parents) to intervene when they see a student receiving vicarious information that they are not as successful as their peers. Intervening at this critical juncture can change the message the student is receiving from "I'm not as good as them" to "I can do it too."

Verbal Persuasion

In an attempt to be positive, reinforcing, and supportive, those close to a student—whether they be friends, teachers, or parents—often use various forms of verbal persuasion to convince the student that he or she has what it takes to succeed. Indeed, verbal persuasion *can* serve the purpose for which the well-meaning sender intends: It can convince someone who is uncertain of their abilities that they do, in fact, have the ability to succeed with appropriate effort. Phrases such as "You can do this," "You'll do just fine (or great)," "I have faith in you—I know you're going to do well" are commonplace and meant to be loving and supportive. But, in order to positively affect one's level of self-efficacy, the receiver has to believe that the sender knows what they are talking about. If they do not, the message can have the opposite consequence. For example, let's say our student, Bob, has an important math test this morning. Over breakfast, he is nervous and mentions how he is dreading taking that test. Too often, parents will—with all good intentions—try to quell the nervousness by "assuring" the student that "I'm sure you'll do just fine" or "You're good at this; you don't have anything to worry about" and ending with something like "Go for it, Champ" or some other dismissive phrase. What Bob realizes, though, is that his parents (or teacher or friends—whoever is uttering such phrases) really do not *know* if he will do alright. They do not know the test, they do not know what he knows (or does not know), and thus their cheerleading phrases ring hollow. Moreover, this attempt to make Bob feel confident has likely backfired. Now he is thinking to himself, "They think I'm going to do well, but what if I don't—I'm not sure at all that I will. If I don't, their faith in me and my ability will be destroyed. I will let them down." So, instead of quelling Bob's anxiety about the test, they have probably increased it.

The effective use of verbal persuasion to increase someone's level of self-efficacy requires a level of competence in order to be genuine and accepted as fact by the receiver. Instead of relying on trite phrases such as "Don't worry," or "You'll do great," it is important to be *specific* so as to give yourself credibility in the receiver's eyes. Instead of dismissing Bob's anxiety with a quick "Don't worry, you'll do fine" it is more effective to be honest and factual in order to really *persuade* him of that. For example, Bob could be told, "I know this is an important test. I used to get nervous too. I think you're going to do fine on it because you've shown me that you know the material that is going to be covered on it. You'll see new problems on the test, but you have shown me how you work those kinds of problems and you've mastered it. Do your best, and if there are things on the test that throw you, we will work on them until you get it."

In this example, the speaker is using specifics to convey to Bob facts that he might have overlooked in his anxiety. The speaker is also conveying that even if failure results, constructive alternatives exist and—either way—love and respect for the student is not on the line. No matter what happens, the speaker is not going to be "let down" or "disappointed." It takes time, and it takes thought, to have these types of detailed conversations. The end result, though, can be the difference between actually persuading a student of their abilities and quelling anxiety, and inadvertently doing just the opposite.

Another aspect of "verbal persuasion" is often unintentionally conveyed. Just as verbal persuasion can be used constructively to increase confidence, acceptance, and self-efficacy, it can also be used to send a very different message—especially when it comes to math learners. This happens when a family member, or others who may influence students, inadvertently gives permission to not try, or fail, by saying something like "I'm not a math person either." For instance, our student, Bob, is struggling with grasping a mathematical operation being taught in class. In an attempt to commiserate with Bob's frustration, his parents scan over the homework and say "I could never get this stuff either—I'm not a math person," or "Glad it's not me—I'm too old to learn this stuff again" or "I finally gave up and was thankful I got a C just to graduate." Some parents/family will state that the mathematics being taught is nothing like what was taught and learned when the adults were in school. Therefore, they are unable to help their students and wonder why this "new math" is necessary and hard to understand. What Bob is really hearing, though, is "I don't get it; I've never gotten it, and I wouldn't blame you if you never got it either." In other words, not being a math person or successfully learning the subject is in the "genes." That belief is almost official permission to do little work or to persevere in a subject that is challenging or difficult to use. If questioned by the teacher, a student might even tell them "My mom and dad said they aren't 'math people' either so I guess that's why I'm not either."

Physiological State

The fourth source of efficacy input is one's physiological state or, more simply, what your body is telling you about your level of comfort with your confidence. People who are nervous and agitated, including sweaty palms, racing heartbeat, labored breathing, etc. can sometimes bring about the dysfunction that they most fear (Bandura, 1986). As people act out, physically, the nervousness caused by their own self-doubts, they convey to themselves uncertainty and fear. In problematic cases, students are taught to "breathe," and to focus in positive and constructive ways. In some situations, test examiners play soothing music prior to administering a test. While some environmental strategies, such as manipulating music and lighting, are not easily achieved in a public classroom setting, other strategies are easier for students to accomplish. Such strategies may be simple things like eating and hydrating properly before an exam, getting a good night's sleep the night before, and having internal messages the student learns that are soothing and calming. Whatever parents and teachers can do to spot signs of physiological arousal, and hedge against them, the more they help students avoid negative cues their own bodies are giving out.

Multiple pieces of information impact students as sources for their overall sense of self-efficacy. Those sources can be a learners' moods, parental actions or attitudes, and learners' own physiological cues. Some of this information is significant and remarkable; others happen so quickly and often that they do not register consciously. Combined with the experiences the student has experienced during their educational career, they either continue to strengthen positive self-efficacy beliefs, or their sense of efficacy stagnates or, worse yet, declines. Teachers and families play a pivotal role in the formation and maintenance of self-efficacy levels that lead to academic achievement.

Figure 1.1 summarizes these influences, and their sources, for a student throughout their school day.

Enactive mastery is placed in a larger oval than the other three factors influencing self-efficacy to emphasize its role as the most powerful influencer in the schemata. Whereas teachers, families and peers constitute the majority of "people influences" throughout the day, they are not exclusive. Other influences include extended family members, acquaintances in outside clubs and service organizations, and/or even coworkers for those students working part-time jobs.

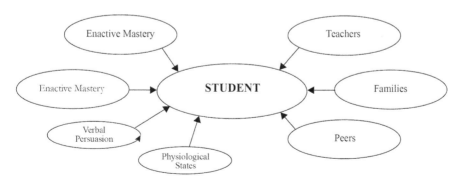

Figure 1.1.

COLLECTIVE EFFICACY

As we work to strengthen a student's level of self-efficacy, we should be mindful of a sense of "collective efficacy" as well. Just as individuals possess internal assessments regarding their belief (and desire) to perform tasks and behaviors, so do groups (Bandura, 1982). Such groups could involve students engaged in a group-learning project, or teachers of the mathematics department of a school, or parents involved with the Parent-Teacher Association or similar community groups dedicated to the welfare of students. Because individuals do not operate in isolation, they continually receive feedback and other cues regarding the strength of their abilities. Students engaged in a group project will more likely engage in constructive, learning behaviors, and successfully complete the task or project, to the extent that they believe themselves capable in doing so and voice that persuasion to other project participants. Teachers, too, will adopt innovative teaching methods to the extent they feel capable, and that it is valued by their district (Hickman, 1993). Parents will feel empowered to step in an offer their feedback and assistance to the extent they feel it will be valued. At the same time, we should be mindful of the things that undermine collective efficacy—some of which are easier to address than others. Rapidly changing environments, the imposition of regulations by external entities like common standards imposed by state (or federal) legislatures, or personnel changes that create a period of uncertainty can all undermine a sense of collective efficacy affecting the classroom, the district, or even the larger community. While "inveterate self-doubters are not easily forged into a collectively efficacious force" (Bandura, 1982b, p. 143), collective efficacy *can* be preserved from external threats by finding ways to bring together conflicting ideas, policies, or situations into focus toward a set of common goals and being sensitive to the effect that these factors have on collective sense of efficacies at play in a student's environment.

Teachers, in particular, operate under a system of "collective efficacy" in addition to their own personal self-efficacy. This, in turn, can affect their students' parents' sense of efficacy and, ultimately, affect the students' sense of efficacy as well. It is critically important that teachers, along with district administrators, understand how collective efficacy works in their building because the dynamics may not be obvious nor understood. Optimally, the triad is fully functional in that each component is consistently engaged, motivated and achieving its goal.

Just as stellar success and cooperation (from colleagues, administrators, parents and students) leads to increased teacher efficacy, the opposite experience can lower efficacy. During the 1940s, teachers were asked what their biggest disciplinary problems were: Chewing gum, making noise, and running in the hall were the top three listed (Bandura, 1997).

By the second decade of the 21st century, the answers include classroom management, disengaged parents, gangs, broken homes, drugs, violence, and teacher competition with students' technological devices such as phones, iPads and iPods. There are also societal forces for which teachers have little or no influence, such as curriculum mandates from state legislatures, and national policies toward standardized testing. Mix with that local and regional demands such as heavy teaching and record keeping responsibilities and large class sizes, teachers can easily feel stretched, powerless, and unappreciated.

Schools operate as social systems among the faculty, not as isolates in their own classrooms. Schools that have a culture of believing that every student can learn, regardless of socioeconomic status, minority status, or home life, tend to have students with greater academic achievement than those who look among the less-motivated student population as uneducable (Bandura, 1995). Judging students as unmotivated or difficult, based on socioeconomic status, home life, minority or immigrant status, or prior grades, only serves as a self-fulfilling prophecy. Those attitudes formed by the faculty in a building-culture can easily generalize to the entire faculty, regardless of the perhaps higher self-efficacy levels of newer faculty members (Ashton, 1985; Bandura, 1997; DeMoulin, 1993).

Faculty of highly efficacious schools take seriously their responsibility in constructing curriculum that achieves high levels of success. They do this by developing challenging assignments and interesting and relevant content that requires mastery and leads to successful completion, while not being so ambitious and difficult as to be intimidating and setting students up for failure. They also think through the tools and activities that enable mastery and success and realize they are a partner with the student in the student learning the content (Ashton, 1985).

Principals of highly efficacious schools are often the academic leader of the building. They are current on instructional methods and promote teacher professional development and the success of the students. These leaders know the students and their parents well, and are sensitive to whatever issues are present in the demographic of the student body. They perceive their jobs as removing obstacles to learning, and giving teachers whatever tools they need to do their jobs better. Principals of less efficacious schools tend to be the chief disciplinarian, whose work involves too-frequent negative interactions with students as well as routine bureaucratic issues like scheduling and lunch/bus schedules. There is less emphasis on the faculty role of instructing and professional development than in more self-efficacious school cultures (Ashton, 1985).

Faculty of highly efficacious buildings reach out to parents and try to make them partners in their child's learning. The more secure teachers are in their content, and the more enthusiasm they have for teaching and their students' learning, the easier it is to get parents involved as partners in the learning enterprise. This type of teacher-parent cooperation mutually enhances both parties' level of self-efficacy (Bandura, 1997). Instead of identifying some parents as "uninterested," efficacious teachers understand that some parents may have had bad experiences in school themselves, or feel intimated by them. They make contact in a way that is approachable, respectful, and nonthreatening. They adjust their conferences to fit the parent's schedule, and even occasionally make a home visit to reinforce the desire for a connection. Most importantly, however, they convey to the parents the belief that their child can do this, and that they are enthusiastic in ensuring their child masters the material. They plan out a way for the parent to reinforce the lessons to help their child learn. They keep up the line of communication so that parents know the teacher is serious and engaged.

Collective efficacy, then, is an important component of the psychological processes operating in the school building, in the home, and in students' minds. Each are reciprocally related in that the students, their parents, and the faculty are continually receiving environmental cues that directly affect each of their levels of self-efficacy. Changing collective efficacy levels can be difficult, especially at the school-building level. Sometimes such changes require a collective reflection by all of the building's stakeholders, including administrators, faculty, and perhaps parents and community leaders as well to figure out best ways to move forward that best serve the interests of student learning. Chapter 4 discusses collective efficacy in detail, and offers practical strategies to examine a building's collective efficacy.

Table 1.2 summarizes the differences between collective efficacy levels of school buildings (Bandura 1995, 1997). This section discusses teacher efficacy from a "collective" standpoint, with teachers viewed as members of a group of professionals in a school building who, together, have formed a collective sense of their efficacy (strong or weak) as a faculty, or even as a district.

In subsequent chapters, we will examine specific strategies teachers and families can use in this process from their unique perspectives. We will also examine ways to assess self-efficacy quickly, for maximum impact. Finally—for teachers—we will examine ways to look for efficacy in the classroom, and explore options for teaching and curriculum that enhance the acquisition of healthy self-efficacy levels.

DISCUSSION QUESTIONS

1. How do you see self-efficacy theory in operation in your classroom and personal life?

**Table 1.2.   Comparison of School Buildings
That Have High and Low Collective Efficacy**

Role	Low Collective Efficacy	High Collective Efficacy
K–12 teachers of math	Teachers largely believe that most students are unmotivated to learn and do not care about math; doubt that parents will assist; have little faith in the administration; have contempt for mandated state standards. Most are burned out and counting the days until retirement.	Believes that every student can learn with the proper instruction; seeks out new strategies to teach difficult concepts; seeks communication with parents; enrolls in advanced coursework or professional development; works with district for resources; investigates new standards and how to meet them.
Principal	Chief disciplinarian; enforcer of rules for students and teachers; bureaucrat; limited contact with students or parents. Cares about the Math Department only to the extent that they do not pull down building scores on standardized tests.	Chief academic officer; engaged with teacher development; knows students and parents; removes obstacles to learning. Actively engaged in math-learning strategies and understands (and can communicate) the importance of solid math instruction to teachers, students and their parents.
Teacher	Believes some students (especially low-income, minority, immigrant) are uneducable; has long-since given up trying to reach these students; goal is to get through another year. Presents material and if students get it, they pass; if not, they fail. Is burned out and frustrated.	Believes all students can master the material with enough guidance and feedback; reaches out to parents often and consistently; restructures lessons if students are having difficulty so that all achieve. Is motivated by the challenges, and constructively plans alternatives to frustrations.
Student	Prefers to work in isolation so that either group does not pull them down, or to be left alone. Doubts his or her ability to master the material and does not care either way. Goal is to just pass to get out of the class.	Prefers cooperative learning to construct and share knowledge; social aspect makes learning fun; believes that the group can learn difficult material faster than the individual. Enjoys learning.
Family	Distrusts, dislikes, or is intimidated by schools and teachers; does not know how to help their student. Does not consider themselves a "math person" and advertises that fact to teachers and their child.	Wants to be a partner with the teacher; appreciates the open communication; believes their input is valued and respected. Believes in their ability to help and encourage their child.

2.   How self-efficacious do you consider yourself to be as a teacher, overall?

3.   How do you rank the self-efficacy levels of your fellow teachers, and students?

4.   For which curricular topics/subjects to do you feel most self-efficacious? Less self- efficacious? Why do you think so?

5.   Based on what you know now, what preliminary thoughts do you have about raising the self-efficacy levels of your students, and yourself?

6.   What strategies have you used to help families increase their child's self-efficacy in one specific curricular area?

7.   What examples of enactive mastery do you find more effective in students' academic success?

GLOSSARY FOR CHAPTER 1

Social Learning Theory.   Developed by Albert Bandura, this learning theory states that human behavior is guided by an interaction between one's thoughts, one's behavior, and the reaction to one's behavior by other people (the environment). People are guided in similar situations, and in future behaviors through this interaction.

Self-Efficacy Theory.   This is a component of social learning theory. Self-efficacy theory states that one is likely to attempt a new behavior if one believes in their ability to successfully perform the behavior (efficacy expectation) and, if performed, that the behavior will lead to a positive or desired outcome (outcome expectation). Levels of self-efficacy are thought to determine perseverance in the face of failure, frustration, and other obstacles.

Enactive Mastery.   A thorough understanding of a behavior and how to perform it properly on command (e.g. dividing fractions or any other mathematical operation). Enactive mastery is the most powerful influence of a person's level of self-efficacy. Chapters 3–6 of this book offer many examples of enactive mastery math activities.

Vicarious Experiences.   The act of watching another person of similar ability successfully perform a desired operation (e.g., one student watching another successfully perform a mathematical operation). Vicarious experiences are the second most powerful influence of a person's level of self-efficacy.

Verbal Persuasion.   The act of encouraging students to try a new behavior and to persevere when attempts are not successful. Examples could be, "You have a good grounding in addition and subtraction. I'll guide you along so you can do this." Or, "No, that's not quite right. Let's see where the mistake is so you can correct it and know next time." Verbal persuasion is the third most powerful influence of self-efficacy.

Physiological States.   Humans react to stress physiologically. These physiological symptoms of rapid breathing, sweaty palms and feeling anxious inform a person that they are nervous and could be in danger of failing, thus preventing someone from trying a new behavior or skill. Spotting anxiousness in students is key to eliminating anxiety and assuring them that you will guide them to success.

Reciprocal Determinism.   Refers to the idea in social learning theory that thoughts, behaviors and others' reactions to the behaviors (the environment) all interact with each other to guide humans to decide whether or not it is safe to engage in a new behavior. This interaction leads to a judgment whether or not the behavior can be performed and, if so, whether it will lead to a positive outcome.

Locus of Control.   A motivation theory suggesting that people attribute outcomes to their behaviors through either Internal or External factors. Those possessing a predominately Internal Locus of Control believe that they, themselves, are responsible for their fate and have control over their environment (e.g., I got an A because I studied hard; I didn't get the promotion because the successful candidate had more experience than I did; I can get what I want if I study hard). Those possessing a predominately external locus of control believe that their fate is controlled by external factors, such as luck or whether others like them, or even the stars (e.g., I got an A because I lucked out and the test had easy questions; or, I didn't get the promotion because the boss doesn't like me).

Collective Efficacy.   The theory that groups of peers (students, faculty, parents) have beliefs about their effectiveness that generalize across the peer group. For example, a group of teachers may feel, collectively, incapable of teaching certain students; students, collectively, may feel ill-equipped to meet curricular demands. Chapter 4 of this book provides detail of collective efficacy and strategies to change it.

REFERENCES

Armor, D., Conroy-Oseguera, P., Cox, M., King, N., McDonnell, L., Pascal, A., … Zellman, G. (1976). *Analysis of the school preferred reading programs in selected Los Angeles minority schools* (Rep. No. R-2007-LAUSD). Santa Monica, CA: Rand Corporation.

Ashton, P. (1985). Motivation and the teacher's sense of efficacy. In C. Ames & R. Ames (Eds.), *Research on motivation in education* (Vol. 2, pp. 141–171). Orlando, FL: Academic Press.

Ashton, P. T., Olejnik, S., Crocker, L., & McAuliffe, M. (1982). *Measurement problems in the study of teachers' sense of efficacy.* Paper presented at the annual meeting of the American Educational Research Association, New York, NY.

Bandura, A. (1977a). *Social learning theory.* Englewood Cliffs, NJ: Prentice-Hall.

Bandura, A. (1977b). Self-efficacy: Toward a unifying theory of behavior change. *Psychological Review, 84*(2), 191–215.

Bandura, A. (1982a). The assessment and predictive generality of self-percepts of efficacy. *Behavioral therapy and experimental psychiatry, 13*(3), 195–199.

Bandura, A. (1982b). Self-efficacy mechanism in human agency. *American Psychologist, 37*(2), 122–147.

Bandura, A. (1986). *Social foundations of thought and action: A social cognitive theory.* Englewood Cliffs, NJ: Prentice-Hall.

Bandura, A. (Ed.). (1995). *Self-efficacy in changing societies.* New York, NY: Cambridge University Press.

Bandura, A. (1997). *Self-efficacy: The exercise of control.* New York, NY: W. H. Freeman and Company.

DeMoulin, D. F. (1993). Re-conceptualizing the self-efficacy paradigm: Analysis of an eight-year study. *Education, 114*(2), 167–200.

Guskey, T. R. (1981). Measurement of responsibility teachers assume for academic successes and failures in the classroom. *Journal of Teacher Education, 32,* 44–51.

Hickman, C. J. (1993). *The structure of instructional criteria in corporate settings.* Unpublished doctoral dissertation, University of Missouri-St. Louis.

Rose, J. S., & Medway, F. J. (1981). Measurement of teachers' beliefs in their control over student outcome. *Journal of Educational Research, 74,* 185–190.

Rotter, J. B. (1966). Generalized expectancies for internal versus external control of reinforcement. *Psychological Monographs, 80,* 1–25.

Zee, M., & Koomen, M.Y. (2016). Teacher self-efficacy and its effects on classroom processes, student academic achievement, and teacher well-being: A synthesis of 40 years of research. *Review of Educational Research, 86*(4), 981–1015.

CHAPTER 2

SELF-EFFICACY
AND STUDENT LEARNING

How does self-efficacy affect students in increasing their knowledge and skills? How can teachers ensure that every student learns? This chapter will focus more on specific teachers, and how their individual levels of self-efficacy affect their attitudes, their performance, and by close-extension, the achievement of their students. What type of teacher is most likely to experience high, versus low, levels of self-efficacy? What influences a teacher's levels? Are levels consistent? How can a teacher's self-efficacy level be raised? Finally, what does the research tell us about the effects of high, versus low, levels of self-efficacy among teachers?

THE EFFECTS OF SELF-EFFICACY
ON TEACHER ATTITUDES AND BEHAVIOR

Gibson and Dembo (1984) and Bandura (1995, 1997) have drawn fairly succinct distinctions between the performance levels of teachers possessing higher, versus lower, levels of self-efficacy. Teachers with higher levels of self-efficacy tend to believe that they can reach even the most difficult student. In fact, such teachers fully recognize the challenges they face and the hardships many of their students have. The common thread these teachers possess is a belief that all students can learn, if given the appropriate amount of time and level of instruction for them. They also believe that they are versatile enough to respond to a wide range of needs that

Learning Mathematics Successfully: Raising Self-Efficacy in Students, Teachers, and Parents
pp. 23–43
Copyright © 2019 by Information Age Publishing

23

surface in their classes. They tend to feel highly qualified in their subject area, have had successful experiences enabling difficult students to succeed, feel an internal reward for their own learning and for being the best teacher possible. They work closely with colleagues to share strategies and other ideas, and they work closely with parents as partners in their child's learning. Teachers with lower levels of self-efficacy tend to be less confident in the mastery of their subject area, tend to not spend extra time with struggling students, are not creative in instructional design of their material, and do not engage parents in the educational scheme of their students (usually because of a cynical view of parents as being uncaring, incompetent, or disinterested). These teachers may describe themselves as being more motivated and enthusiastic about teaching earlier in their career, but students—as a whole—never lived up to their expectations. Not having the skills or development in their toolbox to address these realities, they instead wrote the students off as too challenging. These teachers tend to describe themselves as overly stressed, or burned-out. They feel little, if any, intrinsic rewards or motivation to continue teaching—they do so for the paycheck, or to accumulate years toward their pension, or to reach the few students they perceive as genuinely interested and capable.

Teachers with low levels of self-efficacy are generally happy to stay put in their current position at their current school, as long as they are not held accountable and as long as there is not a leadership change (i.e., new principal or superintendent) who tries to instill enthusiasm and self-efficacy. This does not suggest that this is their reason for not moving on; it means that they are not motivated to do so. If, however, there is a change in school leadership and an efficacious principal comes on board, they will be the ones who roll their eyes, say they have "heard this all before," and write off the new leader as naïve or "green" and bound for failure. These teachers will isolate themselves against change and new ideas by withdrawing from committees, refusing to adopt new ideas or ways of thinking, or arguing that "we've tried this all before and it does not work." Indeed, they will find equally low self-efficacy teachers and reinforce each other's resistance in a variety of ways. Teachers with higher levels of self-efficacy, though, who find themselves in this type of environment, will tend to look for a job elsewhere, in a building that is creative, enthusiastic, and is comprised of faculty who believe as they do—where they can make a difference and a building led by a principal who feels the same way and encourages self-efficacious behaviors among the faculty. It is not surprising, then, that buildings can turn over from either high-level buildings to low-level buildings, and vice versa depending on the leadership that building has.

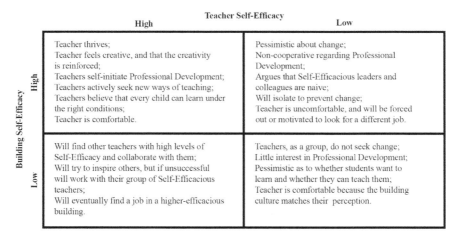

Figure 2.1.   Common traits among teachers in high- and low-efficacious buildings by level of teacher's self-efficacy.

The goal of any teacher, principal or even school board is to strive for high collective self-efficacy in buildings as well as high teacher self-efficacy. As can be seen by the upper left-hand box of Figure 2.1, these environments enable teachers to thrive and feel fulfilled in their teaching role and, more importantly, create a maximum learning environment for students. Environments characterized by low building efficacy and high teacher efficacy, or low teacher efficacy and high building efficacy (the lower left and upper right boxes, respectively), lead to teacher frustration and usually high turnover, both of which adversely affect student achievement. Lastly, even though low teacher and building self-efficacy (lower right hand box) is congruent between teacher and building, it is actually the worst scenario because teachers suffer from a hopeless state of low self-efficacy, and there is no leadership within the building to change that. The adverse consequences on student learning in this kind of environment is obvious.

Donald DeMoulin (1993) addressed some of these issues in an eight-year study of preservice teachers as well as seasoned teachers. His overarching questions pertained to why some highly seasoned teachers continued to be inspiring to students, while others with the same level of experience were less so? Why did some novice students enter the classroom confidently and competently, while others did not? What factors led to these differences? DeMoulin framed his research in self-efficacy theory to explain these differences and offer perspective and recommendations. Building on Bandura's thoughts that self-efficacy was largely derived from enactive mastery, vicarious experiences, verbal persuasion and one's physiological state, DeMoulin found that self-efficacy, in educational settings, was also driven by three components: Motivation, Confidence, and Stress.

1. *Motivation* consists of both *intrinsic* and *extrinsic* factors. Intrinsic motivation refers to those factors that occur within an individual to inspire them to perform. Common intrinsic motivators include pride in doing well, satisfaction that comes from accomplishment, an internal desire to achieve and be the best possible, and an internal work-ethic requiring completion of tasks started and following through on promises. Extrinsic factors are external to an individual, but nevertheless can serve to motivate. Common extrinsic motivators include pay, recognition, opportunities to advance, and respect earned from colleagues and parents. The key for the individual, as well as for the leader (e.g., principal) is to be aware of the motivators for oneself and for the teachers in the building.

2. *Confidence* is comprised of a teacher's knowledge set and skills. Knowledge refers to the facts and content a teacher has acquired in their subject area. Skill refers to a teacher's ability to impart that knowledge in a level-appropriate way to students. Having high levels of knowledge, without the skill to impart it (and vice versa) lessens a teacher's confidence and thus their self-efficacy.

3. *Stress* is comprised of two types: Primary and Secondary stressors. Secondary stressors are minor everyday annoyances that are handled by the teacher personally, such as oversleeping, a sick child, falling behind in grading, or unscheduled meetings and obligations. Usually these are temporary and accommodated throughout the day. In sufficient numbers or regularity, however, secondary stressors can amount to a primary stressor. Primary stressors usually are not handled alone, and can cause a disruption in the teacher's effectiveness and their self-efficacy. Examples of primary stressors include financial difficulties, divorce, death of a loved one, and loss of a job (or a spouse losing their job).

One's placement on motivation, confidence, and stress-scales can vary over time, thus affecting one's level of self-efficacy. DeMoulin (1993) terms this an "efficacy shift" and, optimally, a teacher would "shift" toward higher levels of efficacy with tenure and experience. However, that is not always the case as shifts could occur downward for a host of personal and professional reasons. It is incumbent therefore for teachers to be self-aware about which factors motivate them, be aware of the currency of their knowledge and skills, and be aware of the levels of stress in their lives. Noticing a downward change in any of these areas can lead to adverse effects on self-efficacy. Feeling tired, discouraged, or even burned out can be symptoms of negative shifts in one of these areas. For teachers, being aware of this could hopefully lead them to initiate corrective action (seeking out rewards that matter, or professional development to increase confidence, or finding ways to eliminate stressors). For leaders such as principals, assessing and recognizing teachers' levels of efficacy can inform them as to steps they can take to reverse any downward trends and restore a teacher's enthusiasm for teaching and their students.

In analyzing the self-efficacy strength of 2,640 participants in eight U.S. states, among preservice, novice and experienced teachers, DeMoulin's findings were congruent with Bandura's theory and informs teacher-preparation programs, principals, and teachers themselves on common traits:

- Elementary teachers, both at the preservice and novice level, tended to enter the profession with significantly higher levels of self-efficacy than did secondary teachers. One reason for this might be that elementary methods courses concentrate more on hands-on activities and student-centered learning styles, which may have created a more realistic atmosphere. Secondary methods courses tend to concentrate more on content and be lecture-centered.

- Teachers at all levels who possessed higher levels of self-efficacy, directed attention to all students and gave ample time and attention to struggling students. Teachers possessing low self-efficacy tended to shun low-ability students and focused their time and attention on students whom they believed would succeed.

- Many novice teachers come into the classroom with idealistic attitudes about their ability to make a difference and affect change. After some time in the profession these teachers can become discouraged and drop out. It is important, therefore, for colleagues and principals to be aware of this possibility, and have adequate support systems in place to support and mentor new teachers.

- There were significantly positive correlations between levels of efficacy and a teacher's attitudes toward student achievement and about students themselves.

- There were significantly positive correlations among all levels of teachers between levels of efficacy and a teacher's sense of job-satisfaction, expressions of creativity in the classroom, and seeking out appropriate professional development opportunities.

- Not surprisingly, there were negative correlations between self-efficacy levels and teachers who dropped out within four years of beginning teaching.

Ashton and Webb also found distinctions between efficacious and non-efficacious teachers in the areas of classroom management and instructional strategies. Nonefficacious teachers tended to view their classroom in terms of conflict: Me versus them. To them, their job was to maintain *control* by whatever means necessary. This could come in the forms of rigid "rules" to be observed in the classroom, to publicly embarrassing students who got out of line. While these classrooms might have the outward appearance of "order," there was usually an undercurrent of hostility and tension on both sides of the desk. The root of this rigidity stemmed from teachers' beliefs that "if you give an inch, they'll take a mile" philosophy. One low-efficacy teacher summed it up this way:

> Goodness, the abuse you have to put up with. Well, it's not that you have to put up with it, but it comes back every day. Discipline problems burn you out and make you feel useless. You've already reached the kids you're going to reach ... during the first 5 minutes of class. You spend the next 20 minutes worrying about discipline. (Ashton & Webb, 1986, p. 76)

In contrast, whereas low efficacy teachers' classrooms can be marked by hostility, disruption and conflict, high efficacy teachers' classrooms were "characterized by relative harmony" (Ashton & Webb, 1986, p. 79). That is not to suggest that efficacious teachers did not have student behavioral problems and disruption too. They did, but how they were managed differed markedly. High-efficacious teachers handled student behavior problems quickly, quietly, and directly and moved on. They did not shame the student publicly. Unlike low efficacy teachers, they did not feel these behaviors were a threat to their authority and did not necessarily assume that the student intended to misbehave and disrupt. As such, their findings were that teachers high in self-efficacy experienced fewer disruptions, and their classes had an overall friendlier and relaxed feel. As one highly efficacious teacher summed it up: "It has to be a relaxed situation. I don't like ... a strict, regimented type of teaching. If students are relaxed and the teacher is relaxed ... there is more learning occurring" (p. 79).

THE EFFECT OF TEACHERS' EFFICACY ON INSTRUCTION

Sharp differences between teachers possessing low self-efficacy and those possessing higher levels have been seen (Ashton, 1985; Bandura, 1995, 1997; DeMoulin, 1993). Teachers possessing higher levels of self-efficacy expected students to be attentive and come prepared ready to learn. But, they also possessed a positive, can-do attitude that they conveyed to the class with clear goals for the day and something for everyone to do. They were prepared with a differentiated curriculum, if need be, to accommodate varying learning styles and skill levels of their students. They also stayed on task throughout the period by minimizing off-topic conversations with students, or outside interruptions. These teachers had a positive demeanor, and clear goals for the class that included every student. One teacher was quoted as starting her class periods with a variation of this: "Let's have your attention please, this is going to be a great day. We're going to get a lot done. I don't want anyone to miss a thing" (Ashton & Webb, 1986, p. 85). Highly efficacious teachers set this tone, closely monitor and encourage each student, and overall take a personal responsibility for each student mastering the content—even if it takes some students longer to do so.

Those with low self-efficacy thought the idea of "reaching all students" was naïve and bound to lead to frustration or, as one teacher termed it, "a first year [of teaching] mistake" (Ashton & Webb, 1986, p. 81). Many of these teachers preferred to concentrate on the students they felt they could reach, and who would (or could) learn, and ignore the rest. They became adept at figuring out which students belonged in which category pretty early in the school year, and acted accordingly. Specific teacher-behaviors included calling on less-able students less often, and seldom pushed these students to do their work. In some cases, these less-able students were assigned trivial tasks or assignments to "keep them busy" so the teacher could concentrate on "the brighter ones" (p. 82). Given this scenario, it hardly seems surprising that low-efficacy teachers experienced more disruptive behavioral problems in their classes than did higher-efficacy teachers.

FIVE DOMAINS IN LESSON DESIGN

Recall from Chapter 1 the four most important influencers of self-efficacy: performance mastery, vicarious experiences, verbal persuasion, and physiological states. Knowing what these influencers are, and their order of importance, cues teachers as to how to approach content and instructional design in a way that maximizes a student's confidence and mastery. How that is translated into concrete lesson plans can take many forms, depending on the subject, the students, and the style of the teacher. Dale Schunk (1995) outlined five broad domains for teachers to consider in designing educational experiences that affect student efficacy. Those five domains are goal setting, information processing, models, feedback, and rewards.

Goal setting is an important piece of strengthening self-efficacy. The old adage, "If you don't know where you're going, how will you know when you get there?" speaks to the importance of setting realistic and obtainable goals for your students. As explained in the "backwards design" instructional strategy, we ought to start with the end point and plan back-ward from there, considering how we will get students from where they currently are with a skill or concept to where we hope they will be (Wig-gens & McTighte, 1998). For example, teachers can list the steps needed to be understood for subtraction with regrouping as including space value, trading between places, and recording results in the correct place value column. As steps are achieved, students see progress and become increasingly confident toward mastering additional steps to achieve the final result. To the extent that students can set their own goals, the more powerful realizing the goal becomes. Schunk (1985) experimented with a group of learning-disabled sixth graders on setting goals for a math unit on subtraction. Those able to set their own goals, and achieve them, real-ized higher levels of confidence and self-efficacy compared to goals that were externally set by a teacher or experimenter, or had no goals at all. Importantly, achieving process, or conceptual goals, rather than master-ing only rote procedures leads to higher levels of self-efficacy.

Information processing refers to making sense of the information students receive. Research has found that students' levels of self-efficacy rise when they believe they are capable of learning it, and have a strategy they per-ceive as reasonable for doing so. As students progress academically, they receive feedback (both internally and externally) as to how they are doing and whether they are comprehending the material. If the feedback is pos-itive, this obviously heightens confidence and a sense of self-efficacy. If the feedback is negative, or if the student does not feel s/he is making much progress, this does not necessarily lower a student's level of self-efficacy if the student believes s/he can learn it with a different strategy. Providing var-ious strategies, depending on the subject and the student's skill-level, is key and has been demonstrated to increase skill acquisition in disabled students learning to write essays (Graham & Harris, 1989), teaching children how to do long-division (Schunk & Gunn, 1985), middle schoolers doing various mathematical operations (Zimmerman & Martinez-Pons, 1990), and chil-dren learning subtraction (Schunk & Cox, 1986). To heighten effectiveness, some teachers employ a tactic called *strategy verbalization* (Schunk, 1995) which asks students to verbalize each step of the strategy to focus their atten-tion on it, and to allow them to work systematically.

Models serve as an important function of vicarious learning. To the extent that models (be they teachers or fellow students) vocalize optimism about performing a task—and then their ease of actually doing it— directly affects a student's level of self-efficacy. In addition, research (Schunk & Hanson, 1985) informs us that peers' models (as opposed to teacher models or no models) serve as the strongest source of modeling for learners. Watching peers, who are perceived to be largely equivalent in terms of intelligence and experience, solve math problems formed a stronger source of vicarious learning than watching a teacher solve a problem alone on the board. Creating instructional opportunities for students to showcase their own problem-solving skills are powerful sources of information for the other students in the class.

Feedback is an entity few can deny holds an important place in any instructional-scheme. Indeed, even if teacher-directed feedback is lacking, students continually give themselves feedback as to their progress, which informs them as to their level of confidence and self-efficacy at mastering the material. External feedback (i.e., from the teacher) serves to either reinforce the student's own perceptions, or brings the perception in line with reality. Timing provides information to the student that could be time-sensitive in keeping the student on track. *Attributional feedback* helps the student to realistically determine the reason for his or her success, such as, "You worked hard on this." The ability of students to accurately assess their reasons for success or failure is critical in maintaining, or strengthening, a student's level of self-efficacy. If a student fails at a task, it is better for them to understand that failure resulted from lack of effort than lack of intelligence. *Ability feedback* is also important, especially in early stages of learning a new topic and serves to reinforce the ability to grasp the subject and heightens motivation to continue. While ability feedback is important, attributional feedback is more important in forming levels of confidence and self-efficacy.

Rewards have been controversial in education for years (e.g., Lepper, 1983). Yet, in social learning and self-efficacy theory, rewards can play an important role if done the right way. Rewards, themselves, can be motivating as well as informative (Bandura, 1986). Remember that self-efficacy is an assessment of one's ability to perform a given task *and* the belief that performing that task will lead to a valued-outcome. Those "outcomes" could be viewed as rewards, whether they be intrinsic, such as pride of accomplishment, or even the thrill of learning to do something new and interesting, or extrinsic such as praise from the teacher, or good grades. Both serve to heighten self-efficacy. Schunk's research shows us that rewards tied to effort and accomplishment (as opposed to getting rewarded for just showing up and expending minimal or no effort) are stronger, longer-lasting and serve to benefit a student's self-efficacy. Rewards, then, can be an effective part of an instructional strategy, at the right times, for the right reasons, and under the right circumstances.

INSTRUCTIONAL APPLICATIONS

Several educational leaders have taken the principles discussed thus far and translated them into practice based strategies for teachers to adapt to their specific classroom setting. The following are recommendations for teachers' actions and lesson implementation designed to enhance self-efficacy and, thus, motivation to learn. Among things to do include:

- Planning moderately challenging tasks—tasks that are neither so simple that completing them does not lead to a sense of accomplishment, nor so difficult as to invite certain failure. It is important to assess students' current level of competence and devise realistic goals to achieve during the unit.

- Employ scaffolding learning—sequence strategies that match the struggling-student's skill level, and then assess with formal and informal evaluations as students progress. The incremental successes lead to increased confidence and self-efficacy, allowing students to risk tackling more advanced problems.

- Students' interests: Capitalizing on student choice and interest can increase engagement and serve as a good motivator. Struggling students, especially, can benefit by choices such as assignments, length of lessons, and even topics. Non-struggling students can also benefit by making their own choices. Having students make choices that are appropriate for their level increases motivation. In addition, students begin learning important self-directed learning skills that serve them later in life.

- Reinforcement: Recognize effort and correct use of strategy is important to struggling students. Knowing that their efforts, or persistence, is noticed and leading to learning can be powerful motivators for students to continue time-on-task. If a chosen strategy is not working, continual assessment allows a teacher to amend the strategy so that the students stay on track to achieve the goals of the lesson.

- Feedback: Give frequent, focused, and task-specific feedback to inform learners of their progress. Remember that students will be giving themselves feedback, some of it accurately and some of it inaccurately. Being attentive to their true progress, and providing this type of feedback focuses students on their learning much more effectively than spot quizzes or end of unit exams. Pointing out errors, and then helping them brainstorm the process to arrive at the correct problem is better than just pointing out the error and "deducting points." Indeed, processing errors with students—having them vocalize what they think they did correctly and incorrectly—allows them to analyze future performance more effectively and allows them to better find (and correct) future math errors (Margolis & McCabe, 2006).

- Encourage students to try. This falls into the verbal persuasion part of Bandura's self-efficacy theory, and part of the key to doing this well is informing students (especially struggling students) that success is likely so long as they make the effort.

- Stressing recent successes reminds students that they *can* be successful (with appropriate effort). It is important to tie those recent successes with the task at hand. For example, introducing the multiplication of fractions can seem new and intimidating. However, reminding students that they have learned how to add and subtract fractions successfully can serve to ease their minds enough to begin listening and thinking about the operations involved to multiply them.

- Stressing functional attribution statements reinforce to students the belief that their successes (or lack of success) is closely tied to the effort they expended on the task. Students who feel they "lucked out" on an assignment or math problem, or feel success is anything other than effort are not rewarded for doing a job well done. Conversely, it is important for students to understand that failure is due to controllable things—like time and effort—not to innate ability. Students who have employed incorrect strategies or not put forth effort can easily believe, incorrectly, that they "don't have a math brain" or are generally "stupid" when it comes to math. Teachers need to be vigilant and consistent in conveying the message that effort equals success, not "brains" or "luck."

Taken together, these studies provide compelling evidence that students respond positively to teachers who employ simple self-efficacy-enhancing techniques such as goal setting, sensitivity to prior learning, verbal reinforcements, and modeling. Additionally, teachers themselves are reinforced by achieving greater success in the classroom and engaging students with meaningful time-on-task activities.

Teachers, though, are only a piece of the student's learning environment, albeit a critical piece. The students themselves, and their parents, also play important roles. Knowing about the students' levels of self-efficacy (and also their parents') is a vitally important piece of information for teachers. We have examined where self-efficacy comes from, and how it affects teachers and how those teachers can modify their own behaviors and instructional strategies to increase their students' levels of self-efficacy and their students' academic achievements. Now we turn to the students themselves, followed by a brief discussion on parental efficacy.

Table 2.1.   Instructional Strategies Increasing Student Self-Efficacy

Instructional Strategies
• Reviewing lesson accomplishments from the previous day, posting the current lesson's objectives prior to instruction, drawing attention to the lesson objectives as they are covered, and reviewing the lesson objectives at the end of the lesson.
• Asking students to record each day on a calendar something new they learned that day or something at which they excelled.
• Prompting students who perform poorly or attribute their failures to lack of effort and encouraging them to try harder.
• Drawing students' attention to their growth and complimenting them on their specific skills.
• Using student models early to demonstrate some aspects of a lesson to remind them that other students like themselves are mastering the material and therefore they can master it also.

Source: Siegle and McCoach (2007, p, 279).

EFFECTS OF SELF-EFFICACY ON STUDENT ACHIEVEMENT

Research on student-efficacy has occurred since shortly after Bandura first proposed his self-efficacy theory in 1977. It is beyond the scope of this book to critically analyze each study, but it is important to highlight some significant findings as well as to highlight some trends, or commonalities, in the findings.

Few would argue that childhood and adolescence are not complex times in a child's life. Today's youth are bombarded by a host of sometimes conflicting stimuli. Pressures from family, friends, social networks, and other extracurricular activities vie for a student's attention—along with their teachers and the academic demands the teachers place. Unlike previous generations, today's youth must also integrate a dynamic technology into their existence that allows them to tap into incredible knowledge-base resources, but also provides ample opportunity for diverting attention away from learning and its associated schoolwork.

Research on student self-efficacy has taken several forms, including discovering common elements of their self-efficacy as well as investigating whether the general principles of self-efficacy apply equally to males versus females, younger versus older students, American versus foreign cultures (for example, see Hyang-Hwang, Choi, Lee, Culver, & Hutchinson, 2016), low-ability versus high-ability students, and at-risk versus non-at-risk students.

DeMoulin (1993) verified certain common characteristics of the effect of self-efficacy on today's student. In his study of high school students, positive correlations existed between student efficacy and student achievement, teacher efficacy, attitudes toward teachers, attitudes toward peers, and learning. An inverse correlation existed between a student's level of self-efficacy and severity of discipline problems and absenteeism. While discipline problems and absenteeism may point toward low levels of self-efficacy, the underlying problems causing these behaviors could easily be more serious or severe. Teachers, in general, are not trained to observe students 24 hours a day, nor are they necessarily qualified to make sophisticated psychological diagnoses regarding individual students. These findings, confirmed by other researchers as well, provide merely a snapshot of common behavioral traits of students possessing higher, and lower, levels of self-efficacy and should not be construed as a diagnostic tool for sometimes complex issues involving a student.

HOW SELF-EFFICACY AFFECTS MATHEMATICS INSTRUCTION

Several studies have investigated the role of self-efficacy in learning mathematics. Nicolaidou and Philippou (2003) studied 238 fifth-grade students' attitudes toward math and their levels of self-efficacy. While attitudes toward math were positively correlated with math achievement, the strongest positive correlation was between a student's level of self-efficacy and math achievement. Not surprisingly, they also found a correlation between attitudes toward math and self-efficacy. These results strongly mimicked the results of Pajeres and Miller (1994) who found math self-efficacy was a better predictor of problem-solving ability than was one's self-concept in math, the perceived usefulness of math itself, one's prior experiences in math, or gender. Likewise, Pajeres and Graham (1999) identified self-efficacy as an isolated and independent contributor to math success, while also finding no differences between efficacy levels of girls versus boys in middle school. They did, however, find differences between the efficacy levels of gifted students versus regular students, with regular students having a lower efficacy concept and being less accurate in the efficacy perceptions by being overconfident. Pajeres and Kkranzler (1995) had previously found instances of overconfidence in regular students taking high school math courses, scoring even higher on self-efficacy scales than undergraduate mathematics majors. As the authors point out, Bandura (1986) did caution that assessments of self-efficacy strength becomes more accurate with age and experience. Interestingly, those students in more advanced high school math courses tended to be more accurate in their assessments than did those in lower-level classes.

Usher (2009) performed an extensive qualitative study investigating the sources of middle school students' self-efficacy in mathematics. Consistent with other findings, Usher discovered that students who had higher levels of self-efficacy felt more confident and performed better in math classes as opposed to students with lower levels who recounted struggles and failure in attempting to learn math. The most powerful influence on self-efficacy was mastery experiences, consistent with Banduran theory. However, the qualitative nature of this investigation allowed the researcher to delve more deeply into the thoughts and rationale of her subjects. One student explained that his source of self-efficacy in math came from his father, who continually explained to him that he (the father) was "not a math person" but that his son was smarter than he was and he wanted him to excel in school and go far in life. Instead of accepting his father's perception as being "not a math person" as an excuse to not try, it actually enhanced this student's self-efficacy and determination to achieve where his father had not.

Stevens, Olivarez, Lan, and Tallent-Runnels (2004) investigated the role of mathematics self-efficacy and motivation in mathematics among international groups. Even when groups scored similar levels of self-efficacy in mathematics, some foreign students scored lower in self-efficacy and lower in mathematical achievement, even when ability was controlled. Regardless of the findings of this specific study, the important lesson is that different students, belonging to different cultures, may not have the same environments of the dominant culture and their needs for certain types of efficacy sources (e.g., verbal persuasion, reduction of anxiety, or vicarious learning) may vary from group to group and individual to individual. Studies across cultures are continuing, and while most reaffirm the basic tenet that self-efficacy is closely tied to academic achievement, the sources of that self-efficacy can vary from culture to culture, with some cultures needing more of one source than another.

Interestingly, students with teachers of high self-efficacy experienced higher perceived mathematical ability during their last year of elementary school, and they found an even stronger relationship between teacher efficacy and student perception of performance during the first year of middle school. These students perceived math as less difficult and expected to do better at math in the future than those students with less efficacious teachers. In addition, students who went from high efficacious teachers in elementary to low-efficacious teachers in middle school saw a significant decline in their perceived abilities, and judged the content as more difficult than their peers who had higher-efficacious teachers. Somewhat surprising were the results relating to high- versus low-achieving students. Lower-achieving students were found to be more sensitive to the teacher's self-efficacy level than were higher-achieving students with these lower-achieving students responding more favorably to increased teacher efficacy. For higher-achieving students, their levels of self-efficacy did not vary greatly regardless of the teacher's efficacy level. This suggests that higher-achieving students may not need the teacher's efficacy to succeed and that the high-achiever's own levels of efficacy may not be as finely calibrated with their teacher's as are students who are more dependent on teacher-assistance and the teacher's ability to vary instruction to meet their needs. Insofar as some schools pair teachers with lower self-efficacy with low-achieving students (Midgley, Feldlaufer, & Eccles, 1989), this could perpetuate a cycle of lower student achievement and high faculty frustration and burnout. These findings suggest that pairing high efficacious teachers with lower achieving students would enable the best chance for the lower achieving students to succeed in math.

Apart from cultural differences in self-efficacy, studies have examined differences between middle and high school male and female students. Lloyd, Walsh, and Shehni Yailagh (2005) specifically investigated sex differences in self-efficacy levels in mathematics among Canadian elementary and middle school students. Despite earlier findings from other researchers that girls lagged behind boys both in mathematics self-efficacy, and in achievement, their findings did not substantiate the earlier findings. As concerted efforts have been made to encourage females to consider excelling in the math and sciences, and consider those valid career options, we would expect the achieve-gap to narrow between the genders. For example, the researchers found no significant differences between boys and girls on either levels of self-efficacy, or their attributions for success. In both instances, high self-efficacious students attributed their success to effort, while low efficacious students attributed their failure to either course difficulty or lack of teacher-help. There were significant differences, however, between the efficacy levels of the elementary versus the middle school students, with elementary students scoring higher on all self-efficacy measures. This could be attributed to either the older students being more accurate in their assessment, and/or the increasingly difficult content in math courses as one progresses through the school system.

Common elements of self-efficacy transcend cultures, age-groups, and gender, namely, the importance of self-efficacy in academic achievement and the sources for that efficacy. Research continues along a broad spectrum of populations in order to differentiate which specific sources of efficacy more commonly apply to which groups and which situations. Understanding the heritage of students, though, provides teachers with considerable information to make more informed decisions to enhance his or her students' level of efficacy. Part of that understanding involves understanding the culture students come from and their home environments. Parents can be powerful allies in teacher's attempts to instill not only the content, but the value of education. Parents can also be critical partners in enhancing their student's level of self-efficacy.

EFFECTS OF SELF-EFFICACY
ON PARENTAL BEHAVIOR AND ATTITUDES

The importance of parents in the child's educational experience cannot be overstated. In many respects, parents are the "child's first teacher" and someone who influences the child well into adulthood. Parents bring culture and structure to a child's life, and they also bring a host of attitudes that are instilled in the child from a young age. While there are usually formal mechanisms whereby teachers interact with parents (e.g., parent-teacher conferences), consistent contact with most parents is not attempted or, in some cases, desired. Yet, these parents' attitudes can directly affect a child's attitude toward school, toward teachers and other figures of authority, and even eventual career choices. Apart from the parent's influence on the child, and their feelings of competence and self-esteem, parents must also wrestle with their own feelings of adequacy in helping their children succeed academically.

Bandura, Barbaranelli, Caprara, and Pastorelli (2001) examined self-efficacy as shapers of children's career aspirations. Through this study, they discovered the important role parents play in shaping these aspirations, by influencing course choices, promoting (and discouraging) various career paths, and providing opportunities and experiences that lend favorable achievements toward those goals. In fact, there was a strong relationship between the strength of the parent's belief that they can play a strong role in the academic development of their child, and how high they set those aspirations. Parents who aspire great things for children act in ways that promote achievement and success. Because children, like anyone else, do not aspire to career trajectories for which they have no ability and are not suited, parents sometimes play an active role in molding the child toward career paths that they, themselves, find rewarding, either inherently or financially.

Parents can also play an active role by continuing to be part of their child's social fabric through the high school years. Parents who do so tend to at least indirectly influence their child's success and choice of career path (Schunk & Meece, 2005).

Teachers can join parents in common goals for the parent's child (Pajares, 2005). While parents look for objective evidence of a child's progress, through report cards and conferences, they are also continually assessing their child's strengths and weaknesses and can bring important information to the teacher's attention regarding family dysfunction, financial problems, or other negative issues affecting a student's confidence and achievement. Parents can also partner with teachers in expressing the right messages to students in consistent ways, messages that instill the common theme of enhancing self-efficacy through mutual goal setting, designing the right level of difficulty, expecting effort and achievement, and also helping the student cope with frustration and failure.

A teacher can also enhance the parent's level of self-efficacy in parenting their child toward success. A parent does not need to be perfect, nor always do the right thing at the right time. But, what they can do is believe that they have the ability to channel this student's future and be fair and trustworthy as an adult authority figure in that student's life. Families will often tell teachers this during parent-teacher conferences, or during specific conversations about a student's progress in math classes. Comments such as "Oh, well we're just not math people, that's why he doesn't get it" are commonplace, and meant to excuse not trying or failing behaviors. Teachers can educate parents on how to talk to their students about learning math. Instead of reinforcing held-beliefs about their own abilities, parents can be educated about how such messages torpedo any chance their student has to achieve. Thus, instead of staying "we aren't math people" a parent can say things like:

> I know these concepts can be difficult to grasp at first, but let's break it down into understandable parts.

> I found advanced algebra challenging too. It didn't come easily for me. I had to work at it and I finally understood it and did pretty well in it.

> Let's see what it is you don't understand and then let's figure out what you can do to understand it. If we remain stuck, I want you to visit with your teacher about it and let me know what he/she says.

> You've grasped math concepts up to this point. You can do this because you've tackled math problems before. I know the problems are getting harder—take your time and brainstorm this. If you really get stuck, we'll figure out how to do it.

These messages constructively get a student past obstacles and failures by acknowledging the difficultly, but also specifically explaining (persuading) them of their abilities, without providing any excuses for lack of effort or giving up.

Here are some common themes parents and teachers can work together on to be consistent and effective for their student:

- Attribute failures to lack of effort instead of lack of ability. Convince them that failure is not the end, but a process toward success.

Everyone fails, and many successes occur after multiple failures. The key is to "fail better next time."

- Be a good model for perseverance in the face of obstacles. For parents that could mean saying "Alright, we didn't get it this time, but we will next time." Having a never-give-up attitude for things that are important conveys volumes to students in also persevering when tasks are difficult, or when life throws obstacles in their way.

- Never explain failures with excuses. Instead, explain failures in terms of lack of effort. In other words, "You *can* do this if you work harder/try a different strategy/get help."

- Help parents build enriching activities that play to the child's strengths and interests, such as membership in a chess club, gardening club, literary circle, and so on.

- Help parents understand what their goals and dreams for the child are, and whether these goals are consistent with the child's strengths and interests. Help parents understand the strengths and interests of the child, too.

- Lastly, help parents understand the four primary sources of self-efficacy and elicit their help in monitoring their child and using mastery experiences, vicarious experiences, verbal persuasion, and physiological states to enhance their child's level of self-efficacy. Parents can do simple things throughout their time together to reinforce the teacher's goal of instilling high levels of self-efficacy in their student and, subsequently, enabling them to achieve academic achievement.

Chapter 5 contains a detailed discussion about parental self-efficacy, including working with parents to increase their own self-efficacy, the importance of parents working with teachers to foster their child's self-efficacy, and strategies to form productive relationships with parents.

SUMMARY

These first two chapters have laid the groundwork of Albert Bandura's social learning/self-efficacy theory that will be the basis for the remainder of the book. Self-efficacy is described as a person's judgment about their ability to perform a specific task, and a judgment on the value of any outcomes realized by performing that behavior. The sources of self-efficacy were discussed as well as the implications of how these sources of information affect instructional design and teacher behaviors. Research findings on the strength of the association of a student's level of self-efficacy to their mathematics academic achievement were provided, as well as research findings regarding the differences teachers can make in a student's overall success by attending to that student's level of self-efficacy. Finally, the importance of keeping the lines of communication with parents open was emphasized in order to provide clear and consistent messages to students regarding their strengths, competencies, and beliefs about their abilities.

In the following chapters, we will provide specific suggestions on how a teacher (or parent) can assess a student's level of self-efficacy, and how teachers can assess their own level. Using tested and reliable measures is critical in obtaining valid results that can be used to gauge where a teacher or student is in their own development of self-efficacy. We then provide sample math lesson units that specifically incorporate strategies to enhance self-efficacy—strategies that emphasize the four prime influencers of self-efficacy. Through these units, teachers can learn simple and proven techniques that not only pertain to the topic of the sampled unit, but can be generalized to most mathematical units.

DISCUSSION QUESTIONS

1. How would you describe the relationship between your level of self-efficacy and your students'?
2. How would you generally describe the level of parental (or guardian) self-efficacy of your students?
3. How would you change your interaction with parents to heighten their level of self-efficacy, and help them raise their child's?
4. How does Bandura's self-efficacy theory match other motivational theories of which you are aware? How is it different?
5. What resources and information do you need at this point to have a comfortable grasp of Self-Efficacy theory to craft strategies to raise it in yourself and your students?

REFERENCES

Ashton, P. (1985). Motivation and the teacher's sense of efficacy. In C. Ames & R. Ames (Eds.), *Research on motivation in education* (Vol. 2, pp. 141–171). Orlando, FL: Academic Press.

Ashton, P. T., & Webb, R. B. (1986). *Making a difference: Teachers sense of efficacy and student achievement.* New York, NY: Longman.

Bandura, A. (1977). *Social learning theory.* Englewood Cliffs, NJ: Prentice-Hall.

Bandura, A. (1986). *Social foundations of thought and action: A social cognitive theory.* Englewood Cliffs, NJ: Prentice-Hall.

Bandura, A. (Ed.). (1995). *Self-efficacy in changing societies.* New York, NY: Cambridge University Press.

Bandura, A. (1997). *Self-efficacy: The exercise of control.* New York, NY: W. H. Freeman and Company.

Bandura, A., Barbaranelli, C., Caprara, G. V., & Pastorelli, C. (2001). Self-efficacy beliefs as shapers of children's aspirations and career trajectories. *Child Development, 72*(1), 187–206.

DeMoulin, D.F. (1993). Re-conceptualizing the self-efficacy paradigm: Analysis of an eight-year study. *Education, 114*(2), 167–200.

Gibson, S., & Dembo, M. H. (1984). Teacher efficacy: A construct validation. *Journal of Educational Psychology, 76*(4), 569–582.

Graham, S., & Harris, K. R. (1989). Improving learning disabled students' skills at composing essays: Self-instructional strategy training. *Exceptional Children, 56,* 241–251.

Hyang-Hwang, M., Choi, H. C., Lee, A., Culver, J. D., & Hutchinson, B. (2016). The relationship between self-efficacy and academic achievement: A 5-year panel analysis. *The Asia-Pacific Education Researcher, 25*(1), 89–98.

Lepper, M. R. (1983). Extrinsic reward and intrinsic motivation: Implications for the classroom: In J. M. Levine & M. C. Wang (Eds.), *Teacher and student perceptions: Implications for learning.* Hillsdale, NJ: Erlbaum.

Lloyd, J. E. V., Walsh, J., & Yailagh, M. S. (2005). Sex differences in performance attributions, self-efficacy, and achievement in mathematics: If I'm so smart, why don't I know it? *Canadian Journal of Education, 28*(3), 384–408.

Margolis, H., & McCabe, P. P. (2006). Improving self-efficacy and motivation. *Intervention in School and Clinic, 41*(4), 218–227.

Midgley, C., Feldlaufer, H., & Eccles, J. S. (1989). Change in teacher efficacy and student self- and task-related beliefs in mathematics during the transition to junior high school. *Journal of Educational Psychology, 81*(2), 247–258.

Nicolaidou, M., & Philippou, G. (2003). Attitudes towards mathematics, self-efficacy and achievement in problem-solving. *European research in mathematics education III* (pp. 1–11). Pisa, Italy: University of Pisa.

Pajares, F. (2005). Self-efficacy beliefs during adolescence: Implications for teachers and parents. In F. Pajares & T. Urdan (Eds.), *Adolescence and education: Vol. 5. Self-efficacy beliefs of adolescents* (pp. 339–366). Greenwich, CT: Information Age.

Pajares, F., & Graham, L. (1999). Self-efficacy, motivation constructs, and mathematics performance of entering middle school students. *Contemporary Educational Psychology, 24,* 124–139.

Pajares, F., & Kranzler, J. (1995). Self-efficacy beliefs and general mental ability in mathematical problem-solving. *Contemporary Educational Psychology, 20,* 426–443.

Pajares, F., & Miller, M. D. (1994). Role of self-efficacy and self-concept beliefs in mathematical problem solving: A path analysis. *Journal of Educational Psychology, 86*(2), 193–203.

Schunk, D. H. (1985). Participation in goal-setting: Effects on self-efficacy and skills of learning-disabled children. *Journal of Special Education, 19,* 307–317.

Schunk, D. H. (1995). Self-efficacy and education and instruction. In J. F. Maddux (Ed.), *Self-efficacy, adaptation, and adjustment: Theory, research, and application* (pp. 281–303). New York, NY: Plenum Press.

Schunk, D. H., & Cox, P. D. (1986). Strategy testing and attributional feedback with learning disabled students. *Journal of Educational Psychology, 78,* 201–209.

Schunk, D. H., & Gunn, T. P. (1985). Modeled importance of task strategies and achievement beliefs: Effects of self-efficacy and skill development. *Journal of Early Adolescence, 5,* 247–258.

Schunk, D. H., & Hanson, A. R. (1985). Peer models: Influence on children's self-efficacy and achievement. *Journal of Educational Psychology, 77*(3), 313–322.

Schunk, D. H., & Meece, J. L. (2005). Self-efficacy development in adolescence. In P. Pajares & T. Urban (Eds.), *Adolescence and education: Vol. 5. Self-efficacy beliefs of adolescents* (pp. 71–96). Greenwich, CT: Information Age.

Siegle, D., & McCoach, D. B. (2007). Increasing student mathematics self-efficacy through teacher training. *Journal of Advanced Academics, 18*(2), 278–312.

Stevens, T., Olivarez, A., Lan, W., & Tallenti-Runnels, M. K. (2004). Role of mathematics self-efficacy and motivation in mathematics performance across ethnicity. *Journal of Educational Research, 97*(4), 208–221.

Usher, E. (2009). Sources of middle school students' self-efficacy in mathematics: A qualitative investigation. *American Educational Research Journal, 46*(1), 275–314.

Wiggins, G., & McTighte, J. (1998). *Understanding by design.* Alexandra, VA: Association for Supervision and Curriculum Development.

Zimmerman, B. J., & Martinez-Pons, M. (1990). Student differences in self-regulated learning: Relating grade, sex, and giftedness to self-efficacy and strategy use. *Journal of educational psychology, 73,* 485–493.

CHAPTER 3

MATHEMATICAL SELF-EFFICACY AND THE STUDENT

In the previous chapters, we learned that there were four primary sources of self-efficacy in students, in order of importance:

- *Enactive Mastery*: Proving to yourself that you can accomplish a task by actually doing it.
- *Vicarious Experiences*: Watching someone else whose abilities and experiences are similar to yours (such as a fellow classmate) successfully perform a task.
- *Verbal Persuasion*: Encouragement and feedback from those whom the student respects, including teachers, parents, and fellow classmates. This can be especially powerful when coupled with success—however slight or incremental the success is.
- *Physiological States*: A student's perception of their level of anxiety—are they nervous, afraid, sweaty, and/or does their heart pound when confronted with a math problem? Or, are they calm and focused when tackling a math problem?

This chapter explores the importance of self-efficacy in the K–9 student and identifies symptoms of low self-efficacy. We discuss teachers' assessment strategies that can be applied quickly and efficiently. Questions and curricular considerations to raise students' self-efficacy levels, such as what to assess, when, and how often will be explored.

Learning Mathematics Successfully: Raising Self-Efficacy in Students, Teachers, and Parents
pp. 45–69

The Importance of Students' Self-Efficacy.   Self-efficacy is a gauge that can inform teachers of their students' confidence in learning mathematics content. Students who do not believe in their ability to solve examples and problems are often frustrated and do not expend the effort needed to grasp and retain skills and understanding (Bandura, 1986, 1997). Teachers can interrupt this cycle of self-doubt and resulting struggles by being aware of their students' levels of self-efficacy and taking proactive steps to heighten them.

The role of the teacher in affecting students' self-confidence cannot be overstated. Teachers, themselves, may have questions as to their ability to heighten even one student's level as well as that of every student. These concerns do have basis in fact, as studies have consistently revealed that students' levels of self-efficacy can correlate with gender (boys being slightly higher in mathematics than girls) can vary with socioeconomic status (with privileged classes exceeding poorer classes) and in national and international settings (Organization for Economic Cooperative Development, 2013). Nevertheless, teachers *can* break through these *a priori* variables of culture, socioeconomic status, and gender and still heighten levels of self-efficacy through thoughtful and determined effort. To do this, teachers must first recognize symptoms of low self-efficacy and then assess levels and respond appropriately to their findings.

Symptoms of Low Self-Efficacy.   Whereas we strongly recommend assessing students' levels of self-efficacy as a matter of practice, there are behavioral symptoms which may indicate low levels of self-efficacy. Importantly, there is a stark difference between boredom and a not caring attitude and self-efficacy. Boredom usually stems from two origins. The first can be described as students feeling as if they know the content already and so repeating the exercises again and again is not interesting. Another possibility is that students believe the content gap between what they know and what is being taught is so wide that they tune out. These examples of boredom and attitude are not related to self-efficacy. They suggest other factors in play to which teachers should be sensitive in addressing. Spotting symptoms of low self-efficacy requires sensitivity to verbal and non-verbal cues. Table 3.1 illustrates some examples of low self-efficacy symptoms versus high self-efficacy symptoms.

Teachers can note these cues and modify their delivery accordingly— even on the spur of the moment. Sometimes, a teacher will ask the class "Where did I lose you?" or the reflective, "You seem lost or confused, let's clear this up." These types of informal formative assessments can steer the teacher in the right direction and avoid dampening levels of self-efficacy. But, they are not fail-safe guarantees, especially if teachers do not have a clear idea of the self-efficacy levels of their students.

Table 3.1.   Low Versus High Self-Efficacy Student Cues

Student Cues	Low Self-Efficacy	High Self-Efficacy
Verbal student cues	• "I can't" • "I'll never get this" • "I'm lost" • "This is too hard for me" • "I'm no good at math"	• "I got that, but not this" • "I followed you up to here" • "Let me make sure I got this" • "I don't know that I get this, can you explain it again?" • "I'll get it—I just need time to think about it (or practice)"
Nonverbal cues	• Yawn or putting head down • Anxious looking/fidgeting • Blank stare • Irritation/obvious frustration	• Taking notes • Wide-eyed paying attention • Nodding agreement • Nonanxious/calm

Gauging the students' levels of self-efficacy is a critical piece in determining their comfort and confidence levels prior to beginning either a math class or a unit within that class. Fortunately, assessing self-efficacy is relatively efficient and the benefits for doing so can be enormous. Recall that self-efficacy refers to one's belief in their ability to perform a specific behavior, and that there is a positive outcome for doing so; in other words, one believes in their ability to perform, and that performing is worth doing. Both pieces are important to creating, in an individual, the idea that they can (and should) learn a specific behavior (i.e. adding fractions). If the potential outcome is ignored, motivation to learn can decrease. For example, students may believe that they can learn the operational procedures of adding fractions, but without an understandable outcome (point), then it becomes difficult to persist. When students are not initially successful or become frustrated with increasingly difficult problems they are solving for little apparent reason, learning is stymied. A critically important strategy for improving students' interest and conceptual understanding is to promote the relevance of mathematics content. Using examples that justify how mathematics is used in daily life, reasons for learning the content and understanding why it contributes to positive outcomes (i.e. understanding percentages to shop with accurate information, using maps correctly, measuring, cooking and sewing with right measurements) all contribute to raising levels of self-efficacy.

Assessing students' levels of self-efficacy, then, requires an evaluation of their beliefs about their ability to apply new mathematical concepts and their beliefs about whether learning to do so provides positive outcomes and connections to their own experiences. Here are sample questions that can be asked of students; some rewording may need to occur to adapt to the grade level of the student. Some teachers design a Likert scale of *strongly agree* to *strongly disagree*, while others provide a yes-no option. It does not matter, as long as the responses in whatever form are considered useful to the teacher.

1. If I work hard enough, I will be able to make a good grade in this course.
2. I can learn how to _____.
3. If I get confused with this course, I feel free to ask my teacher for help.
4. I know what to do if I get confused.
5. I know why I am learning _____.
6. I can do the work in this class, even if it is hard.
7. I believe that if my friends can do the work, so can I.
8. I have been successful at math before, even if I had to work hard to get it.
9. Other than earning a grade, I see the value in learning _____.
10. I know what to do if I get stuck on a problem.

These questions tap into students' belief-systems and provides a glimpse into students' beliefs before the lesson (or unit) begins. Using this knowledge, the teacher can more easily provide instructional strategies that either reinforce positive levels of self-efficacy or strategies that negate student preconception about dread or failure. This assessment also clues the teacher in on specific students who may be vulnerable to failure due to low self-efficacy. In this way, targeted strategies for the whole class or a small group of students, can be applied to provide a boost to self-efficacy levels.

In the preceding list of 10 questions, #5 and #9 deal with perceived outcomes, including whether or not the student understands the importance of the mathematics topic being studied. As well, the questions provide assessment of students' belief in their ability to either perform the operations of the course, or have strategies in mind to overcome obstacles or other frustrations (e.g., ask the teacher for help or work harder). Teachers should consider the following questions:

*   "Does the student believe he/she can do the work?"
*   "Does the student have a plan when they run into difficulties?"
*   "Does the student understand why it is important to learn the content?"

These initial questions are provided as a basic pretest before beginning the lesson or unit. Frequent formative assessments and feedback are very useful for measuring levels of confidence and interest. Spot assessments, such as the teacher asking the class, "how are you doing?" and "are you getting this?" or "what is confusing you?" provide instructors an understanding of students' mood and confidence relative to the material. A posttest is administered with similar questions, though worded in the past tense, to gather evidence that self-efficacy has been (or was not) heightened when the lesson or activity is finished. Asking students if they felt they passed an assessment because of their hard work, or good luck, or if they feel they can solve a problem when asked, informs the teacher as to whether or not students believe in their ability to solve problems as opposed to being successful by chance or luck. A question such as "How can I or will I use the mathematics I learned in school in my everyday life?" informs the teacher as to whether or not the student has internalized the value of the content. The teacher strives for evidence of increased self-efficacy such that the student now has improved coping strategies to develop concepts and recall procedures.

The following section offers suggestions for increasing self-efficacy by attending to instructional methods that encourage students' active learning. Methods for teaching major mathematics content areas, such as place value, whole number concepts and computation, measurement, fractions and decimal values will be described. We also discuss direct instruction, cooperative grouping, and flipped classrooms and how these methods, overlapped with these topics, dovetail into the four sources of self-efficacy in students: enactive mastery, vicarious experiences, verbal persuasion and physiological traits.

INSTRUCTIONAL METHODS TO ENACTIVELY INTEGRATE SELF-EFFICACY IN MATHEMATICS

Teaching students effective to understand and retain content, as well as maintain a positive attitude toward learning mathematics has been studied and researched for decades in the United States. A common finding in professional recommendations, related to achievement, is that students learn best when they are active and engaged, as well as frequently encouraged by instructors and families (Kilpatrick, Swafford, & Findell, 2001). Toward these ends, researchers and practitioners have identified five curricular strands that establish a strong mathematics foundation. They are:

- conceptual understanding: the comprehension of ideas,
- procedural fluency: flexible and accurate skills and procedures,

- strategic competence: ability to formulate and solve problems,
- adaptive reasoning: capacity to reflect and evaluate one's knowledge and ability to reason, and
- productive disposition: a habitual inclination to make sense of and value what is being learned.

When experiencing instruction founded on the elements listed above learners are more able to advance to higher levels of self-efficacy, achievement and academic success (Kilpatrick et al., 2001).

Using the strands as a curricular framework, the U.S. governors, academic organizations, and individual states' educational agencies developed mathematics standards meant to specifically guide mathematics content instruction and assessment. This K–12 framework is known as the Common Core Standards for Mathematics (National Governors Association Center for Best Practices & Council of Chief State School Officer, 2010). They outline, grade by grade, the expected content knowledge students should know and be able to do. As well, eight professional standards for the methods of teaching mathematics to promote higher level thinking, reasoning, numeracy and productive dispositions were identified and are termed the Common Core Standards of Mathematics Practice (National Governors Association Center for Best Practices & Council of Chief State School Officer, 2010). The standards are the following:

- *Make sense of problems and persevere in solving them.* Students make conjectures about the form and meaning of the solution and plan a solution pathway rather than simply jumping into a solution attempt.
- *Reason abstractly and quantitatively.* Students create a coherent representation of the problem at hand; consider the units involved; attend to the meaning of quantities ... and flexibly use different properties of operations and objects.
- *Construct viable arguments and critique the reasoning of others.* Students understand and use stated assumptions, definitions, and previously established results in constructing arguments.
- *Model with mathematics.* Students apply the mathematics they know to solve problems arising in everyday life, society, and the workplace.
- *Use appropriate tools strategically.* These tools might include pencil and paper, concrete models, a ruler, a protractor, a calculator, a spreadsheet, a computer algebra system, a statistical package, or dynamic geometry software.

- *Attend to precision.* Students communicate precisely to others. They try to use clear definitions in discussion with others and in their own reasoning.
- *Look for and make use of structure.* Students look closely to discern a pattern or structure.
- *Look for and express regularity in repeated reasoning.* Students notice if calculations are repeated, and look both for general methods and for shortcuts.

Each of these practices can be incorporated through hands-on, pictorial and symbolic representations of mathematics that are relevant and reasonable. As students engage in making sense of mathematics, learning is facilitated by connecting content to previous learning and sharing results; students become more self-efficacious.

Enactive mastery involves the principles of "model with mathematics," and "use appropriate tools strategically." As mathematics concepts are learned by actively engaging with materials and drawings, students are constructing their conceptual understanding to remember the rules and procedure. For example, students often learn to add and subtract fractions with different denominators by first finding the common one. Studying multiplication and division of fractions follows the first two operations. A common error is that learners apply the same rules to multiplication and division of fractions that they did to addition and subtraction, finding the common denominator in all cases. These misunderstandings signal that learners' conceptual understanding, reasoning, and strategic competence are weak because the solutions are not accurate. Confusion may lead to students believing they "can't do math."

Vicarious experiences involve learning from others as students "make sense of problems and persevere in solving them, reason abstractly" and "Construct viable arguments and critique the reasoning of others" (National Governors Association Center for Best Practices & Council of Chief State School Officer, 2010). These experiences are manifested as students share their reasoning and solutions with others in class discourse sessions. As well, students learn from others "viable arguments/reasoning" and then decide whether or not classmates are correct or not and why. In general, students profit from explaining their thinking to other classmates and watching others problem solve. Number sense is shared and can lead to students building confidence in their ability to learn and use mathematics.

Verbal persuasion involves all mathematics standards. As teachers and students encourage learners to focus on the structures, reasoning, problem solving and patterning in mathematics, students move to higher levels of thinking and achievement. Students are persuaded that mathematics is relevant, important and sensible as they increase understanding, succeed in small steps forward and receive consistent and frequent feedback. Students make progress in mathematics when provided consistent and continual, personalized assessment (Van de Walle & Karp, 2012).

Each of the facets in Bandura's framework are described in the next section with specific activities and materials that integrate the three components in mathematics instruction.

ENACTIVE MASTERY

Educational research and practice have emphasized that hands-on, active and experiential emphasis in mathematics lessons are effective in students' success (Van deWalle, 2012). These teaching strategies, based on the five learning strands and standards of practice, directly engage students in their own learning and help them understand concepts by making sense of them by making sense of them with materials and activities (National Governors Association Center for Best Practices & Council of Chief State School Officer, 2010).

When new lessons and/or units are introduced, students develop conceptual understanding using hands-on materials, or manipulatives. These are physical or virtual models to touch, move and observe the mathematics ideas they represent. Learning mathematics developmentally, with items such as counters, fraction strips, algebra tiles, geometric shapes, place value blocks and dot paper, enables students to develop ideas that are reasonable and accurate. Students can make sense of numbers and mathematical ideas by moving the objects, drawing them and constructing their own thinking about the mathematics process. Examples of enactive experiences that lead to mastery are described below.

Addition and Subtraction: Developing Concepts and Retaining Procedures

Addition/Subtraction Process: Joining and Removing Sets

Addition is an operation representing the joining of physical objects or abstract ideas (i.e., thoughts, choices, quantity, etc.); subtraction is an operation representing the removal of the objects or abstractions. These operations are modeled when students use physical counters to join, for example, 8 counters with 4 counters, to find the total amount counted is 12 counters and remove 4 counters from a set of 12 to find that 8 objects remain. The objects can be thought of as pumpkins or cookies or baseballs to make them more relevant and fun to discuss in making up examples.

Drawings objects in groups also aids students in recognizing what addition and subtraction operations mean—the joining and separating of sets. Drawing groups or sets of objects encourages number awareness that an addition sentence, 8 + 4 = 12 or 4 + 8 = 12 can also be interpreted as subtraction, 12 – 4 = 8 and 12 – 8 = 4. Examples are shown in the figures.

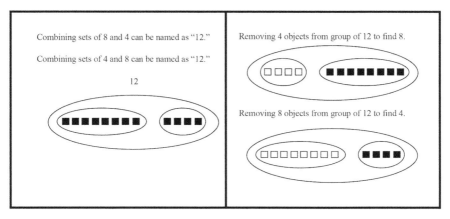

Figure 3.1.   Example of representing addition/subtraction processes.

Understanding and retaining basic facts facilitate using procedures or algorithms for adding, subtracting, multiplying and dividing. Addition facts are the 100 combinations of one digit and one digit of 0 to 9. There are also 100 subtraction facts for the combinations of 0 and 9.

These facts are understood and remembered in relation to fact families. Students model each fact with objects and then record the facts they constructed (seen in Figures 3.1 and 3.2), as done with "8, 4, and 12, "and" 9, 5, and 14.

8 + 4 = 12	12 - 8 = 4
4 + 8 = 12	12 - 4 = 8

9 + 5 = 14	14 - 9 = 5
5 + 9 = 14	14 - 5 = 9

Figure 3.2.   Examples of addition and subtraction fact families.

Forming sets provides students a visual way to incorporate number sense, fluency and number relationships. Students find that memorizing the facts because logical and follows patterns that can be remembered.

Multiplication and Division:
Developing Concepts and Retaining Procedures

Students draw arrays to model the operations of multiplication and division. Arrays are an arrangement of objects, pictures, or symbols in adjacent columns and rows, as seen in Figure 3.3. When arrays are built with counters or drawn, students can see them as a box of square objects or floor tiles or ceiling tiles that measure 3 squares in each column and 4 squares in each row or 4 squares in each column and 3 squares in each row as seen in Figure 3.3.

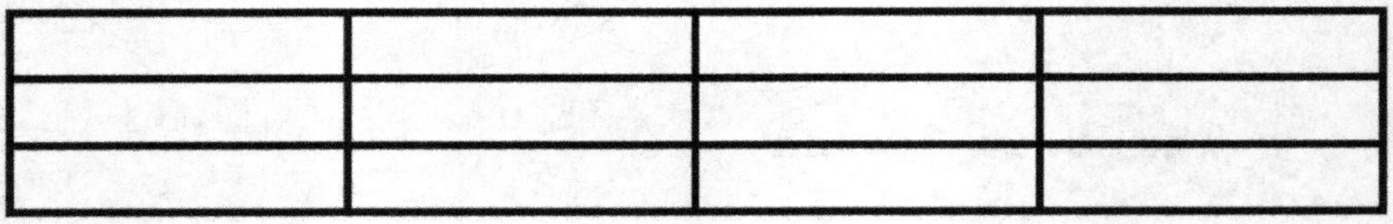

Figure 3.3.

To understand what the multiplication process represents, record the total number of boxes in a number sentence:

4 columns of 3 rows is the same amount as 12

3 rows of 4 is the same amount as 12.

The term, "groups of" can be represented by an "×" sign. The phrase, "is the same amount as," is noted with the equal sign symbol, "=." The resulting number sentences are "3 × 4 = 12" and "4 × 3 = 12." One can also see and discuss the relationship of multiplication to finding the area of a rectangle.

The ÷ symbol will represent the process of thinking that 12 can be shared or divided into 3 equal groups of 4 or 4 equal size groups of 3. Whereas 3 × 4 = 12, 12 shared or divided in 4 equal groups is 3, as seen in the array. Students think of multiplication as equivalent groups of the same amount and division as sharing those items in equivalent groups. An example of a multiplication and division fact family is then written as in Figure 3.4. With this preparation of understanding relationships, students can more successfully memorize basic facts of all four operations.

4 x 3 = 12	3 x 4 = 12
12 ÷ 3 = 4	12 ÷4 = 3

Figure 3.4.   Multiplication/division fact family.

There are 100 multiplication basic facts. These are all combinations of 0–9. However, there are only 90 division facts (example: 12 ÷ 3 = 4) because there are 10 multiplication facts that would involve division by 0. The latter is an undefined fact.

Place Value and Whole Number Computation

Place value concepts depend heavily on the ideas of "trading." The value of 100 can be traded for 10 tens, 10 tens can be traded for 10 ones, and so on. These concepts underlie the basic algorithmic procedures to rename and compute for addition, subtraction, multiplication and division (Van de Walle, 2012).

Students actively engage in understanding the procedures by first using base 10 blocks to trade and represent quantities. The numeral "100" is represented by a block with these markings of 100 squares. The entire square block is called a "flat" and found in Figure 3.5.

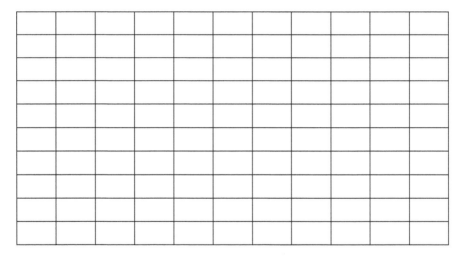

Figure 3.5.   Base 10 flat representing 100 units.

The numeral "10" is represented by a block with these 10 division markings. It is often called a "rod."

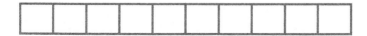

Figure 3.6.   Base 10 rod representing 10 units.

The numeral"1" is represented by a block like this and called a "unit."

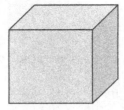

Figure 3.7.   Base 10 cube representing 1 unit.

Students explore the blocks to fit 100 units on the flat, 10 rods on the flat, and trade 10 units for a rod. This trading and hands-on experience is essential to visualizing the quantities represented and successfully renaming them when computing. The number of place value blocks in the example above are modeled on the place value chart. They are then used to solve for a reasonable solution.

Nathan is recording the number of yards he runs at each track meet for 2 weeks to complete his physical exercise class assignment. Here are the distances he ran:

Week 1: 24 yards
Week 2: 13 yards

How many yards did Nathan record that he ran in the 2 weeks?

Place Value Chart

Tens	Ones
2 tens	4 ones
1 Ten	3 ones
3 tens (combine the groups of rods)	7 ones (combine the groups of one units)
3	7

Sum is 37 yards.

Figure 3.8.   Place value chart for addition: 24 + 13.

Enactive mastery of renaming (or borrowing and carrying) will help students build a foundational understanding of place value and its importance when solving examples and retaining the procedures.

Math problem: $\begin{array}{r} 23 \\ \times\ 5 \end{array}$ can be written as $\begin{array}{r} 20+3 \\ \times\ 5 \end{array}$

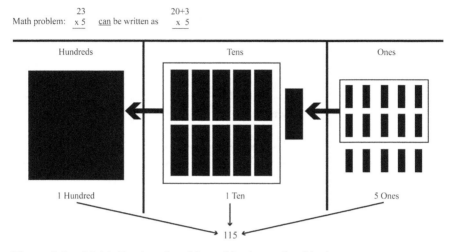

Figure 3.9.   Multiplication algorithm with place value blocks.

Math problem: $\begin{array}{r} 45 \\ +\ 38 \end{array}$ can be written as $\begin{array}{r} 40+5 \\ 30+8 \end{array}$

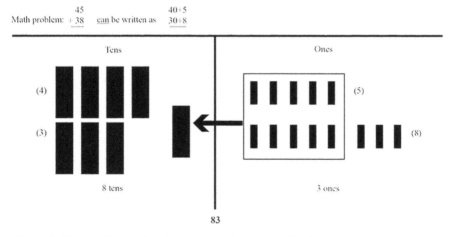

Figure 3.10.   Addition algorithm using place value blocks.

Decimal Numbers: Place Value and Comparing

Decimal place value is a critically important concept, as it was with whole numbers. Students use 100 grids to understand and connect the value of tenths, hundredths and thousandths to previously learned fractions and decimals, and later, to percent. Learners draw grids to represent the decimal values. The figures below indicate how students mark a diagram to connect the concept of part of a whole represented by fractions to the equivalent decimal notation. It is helpful to relate tenths to dimes and, later, hundredths as pennies, as an everyday connection. Students discuss the fact that 10 dimes are the same value as one whole dollar and each dime represents one tenth of that whole.

1/10	2/10	3/10	4/10	5/10	6/10	7/10	8/10	9/10	10/10
0.1	.02	0.3	0.4	0.5	0.6	0.7	0.8	0.9	1.0

Figure 3.11.   Decimal numbers.

Representing hundredths happens as students actively mark a 100 square grid with the fractions and equivalent decimals they represent (see Figure 3.12).

Students need to understand that decimal points serve to separate whole numbers and decimal values and their place depends upon the size of the numbers. Decimal places represent smaller quantities as the numerals extend to more places just as whole numbers represent larger quantities as the numerals extend to more places. Place value charts for tenths, hundredths and thousandths are important, just as the charts were for whole numbers. The following illustrates a decimal place value chart and decimal representations. A common error is that students mark 10/10 as 0.10 and 10/100 as 0.010. These numerals can be confusing. Marking the grids to notice equivalencies presents a visual and engaged way to understand which decimals are the same value and which are not. Understanding that 10/10 = 1.0 and 10/100 = 0.1 is an integral concept to learning to order decimals and compute when adding, subtracting, multiplying and dividing decimals.

Measurement

Measurement is a topic in mathematics that many U.S. students struggle to understand and use (Zacharos & Chassapis, 2012). Students need to experience actual measuring, converting one measure to another and using the tools of measurement to understand what they are finding about an object. For example, this list of activities will provide an active,

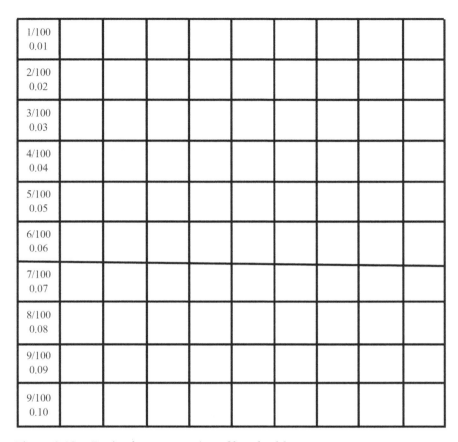

1/100 0.01									
2/100 0.02									
3/100 0.03									
4/100 0.04									
5/100 0.05									
6/100 0.06									
7/100 0.07									
8/100 0.08									
9/100 0.09									
9/100 0.10									

Figure 3.12.   Decimal representation of hundredths.

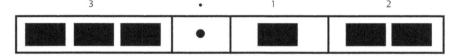

Figure 3.13.   Decimal place value chart.

engaged experience that helps students build the concept of length mea-surement.

• Measure with nonstandard units: Using a piece of string, students compare it to real objects in the classroom and, if possible, at other locations and at home. Matching the end of the string with the end of objects, students find and record which are longer, shorter or the same length as the string.

- Measure with standard units (measuring with commercial tools): Using a ruler, students place it at a zero point next to classroom and other actual items. Students place the ruler at the end of the object and match the end to the 0 end of the ruler. They then mark the number on the ruler that matches the end of the item being measured and report their results. Those are recorded and compared to the length measures found with the string. Students discuss the reasons that nonstandard measures (the string) are not as reliable as standard measures.

Measuring mass, volume, and capacity activities should involve the same conceptual development and reasoning activities. Start with nonstandard units such classroom objects to estimate mass or weight and liquid to measure. Move to standard units of measuring cups and commercial balances to compare and discuss findings.

Fractions: Conceptual Understanding, Naming, and Comparing

Fractions and decimals are topics that can become confusing, rule bound and misunderstood if students do not model them to make sense of their purpose and operations. Fraction strips or tiles are effective models when taught in a sequence that helps students develop the meaning of the symbols, their size and order. For example: students fold a strip of paper in equal parts.

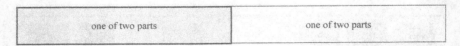

Figure 3.14.   Fraction strips.

After noting and discussing that there are 2 equal size sections in the strip that students folded end to end, one of the sections is shaded. That part will be named a "fraction" because it is the same size as the other part of the strip. Students write "one of two parts" in the shaded section. The blank section, as suggested by students, can also be named "one of two parts" and marked as such. The parts or sections are compared for shape and size and found to be the same. Importantly, students use this hands-on model to understand that when a whole has parts that are all the same size and shape, those parts are named as fractional parts. After students mark the sections as "one of two parts," they connect symbols to the words and pictures. The symbol of ½ is taught and students can identify, using the strips that the numerator, 1, refers to a part of the one strip that is shaded or unshaded. Because the strip is seen with two sections, the denominator of "2" can be related to the number of parts in the whole strip. Students learn that the term "one half" describes the section that is shaded or unshaded and the entire strip is seen as "two halves" because there are two sections and each is the same size and shape. The ratio of 1:2 or "one to two" is also discussed as the relationship of the part that is shaded to the entire strip. The activity continues as students fold and mark sections of fourths, sixths, eighths, and thirds. Fourths are illustrated in Figure 3.15.

one of four	one of four	one of four	one of four

Figure 3.15.   Identifying and naming fourths.

Students are asked to use the previous pattern for ½ and identify the one of four sections with a fraction. Those symbols are discussed and students are asked why 4/4 represents the entire strip. Often students are taught that the "same number over the same number = 1" but have little concept of why that rule is stated. These experiences make sense of what a fractional part means and how fractions relate to each other and the whole.

Equivalent fractions can also be identified and then compared with fraction strips. When a fraction strip is divided into two sections and compared to a strip sectioned off into 4 equal size parts, the ½ section can be seen as matching the same amount of space as two out of four sections or "2/4." As well, two sections of two in the whole strip (2/2) match the same amount of space as 4 sections of 4 in the whole strip (4/4.) Students can determine, from the strips, that 2/2 represents the same space and is equivalent to 4/4. Students write that equivalent statement. 2/2 = 4/4. They can extend that thinking to determine if, for example, 2/2 = 3/3, and so on.

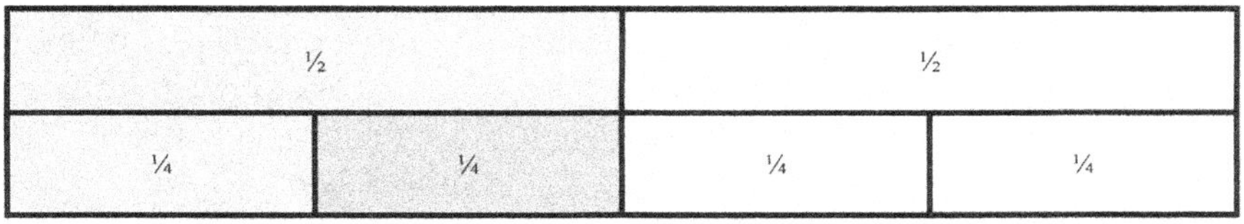

½		½	
¼	¼	¼	¼

Figure 3.16.   Fraction comparison.

VICARIOUS EXPERIENCES:
LEARN FROM OTHERS—FOLLOW THEIR PATTERNS

The term" vicarious learning" or "vicarious experiences" refers to an instructional method in which learners see and/or hear a learning situation (i.e., an observed learner in an instructional situation) for which they are not the addressees and do not interact with the observed learner nor the observed learner's instruction (Schunk, 1985). The learning situation is often presented as video recordings of human interactions or a peer or teacher who is not directly interacting with the student (Bandura, 1986), the definition encompasses live vicarious learning, such as, students watching another student at the front of the class interacting with the teacher. There are three fundamental ways to learn mathematics by observing. These are observations of the

- teacher's presentation and modeling in a classroom;
- classmate's actions and thinking aloud in cooperative groups; and
- student's observations of the teacher in videos and other electronic media.

Direct Instruction

Direct instruction is a teacher-centered instructional approach that is most effective for teaching basic or isolated skills (Kroesbergen & Van Luit, 2003). Students are having a vicarious learning experience as they watch and listen to a teacher explaining a concept and/or procedure, as well as modeling them in the lesson. Direct instruction is followed by more limited teacher involvement and then reduced teacher involvement as students begin to master the material (Van de Walle & Karp, 2012). Teachers' thinking and doing processes can be presented as a whole class instructional strategy or in small groups to target instruction to students' needs.

Students receive immediate oral feedback during teacher centered direct instruction lessons when responding to teachers' questions. For example, in a direct lesson on addition of decimals, teachers present information about lining up decimal points and model examples, talking their way through each problem. Questions are asked and students answer, learning they were correct or not. Students practice a variety of computation examples some involving skills the students have already mastered and some using a new skill. When the students achieve mastery, determined through continuous progress monitoring, teachers move to the next concept but continue, through practice, to reinforce and connect earlier skills (Van De Walle & Karp, 2012).

Cooperative Grouping

Cooperative learning (i.e., learning together, group investigation, student teams-achievement divisions, and teams-games-tournaments) is a generic term used to describe an instructional arrangement for teaching academic and collaborative skills to small, heterogeneous groups of students (Sharan & Shulov, 1989). Group work, or cooperative grouping, has been utilized for many years to enable students to observe other students solve a problem and receive input from the group's suggestions (Johnson & Johnson, 1988). Cooperative group work is structured in mathematics so that all students participate and learn from hearing and observing each other solve problems.

When learning in a cooperative group setting, students start a problem and work it out together. The teacher then provides closure, after students have presented their ideas and shown how they have connected the ideas and added academic vocabulary. Cooperative learning provides opportunities for productive struggle, in which students learn from their mistakes through explanations from their peers and teacher.

One cooperative group strategy is called "red light, green light." Students solve tasks and justify their answer to each other with a table, a graph, and an explanation. One student in the group is designated as the "checker." He/she reviews the answer and explanations. If the group is wrong, the checker calls "red light" to stop, discuss the mistake with the group and fix it. Then the group has a green light. If the group was correct the first time, then the checker calls, "green light" and the group moves on to a different problem. Students are motivated when they don't need the teacher to confirm whether they are right or not. It also empowers students to be responsible for their own learning (Joyce, 2016).

A strategy particularly related to learning from observation is called, "Rally Coach or Pairs Check." Students work on a problem with a classmate. One person talks and explains the problem while the other writes and says nothing. If the writer disagrees, they switch roles. Then the pairs check with the pair across the table from them to see if they got the same answer. This strategy increases accountability for students who do not participate enough when a member of a group of four or more (Joyce, 2016).

"Hot Potato" involves a group of four students using one piece of paper. Each student uses a different colored pencil. They solve one step of a problem and pass the paper to the next person who completes a step,

and so on. Students can look at the paper to determine if everyone is con-
tributing (Joyce, 2016).

Finally, cooperative learning can be used to promote classroom discourse and oral language development. In a cooperative learning activity,
vocabulary and symbolic understanding can be enhanced with peer interactions and modeling (Rivera, 1996).

TECHNOLOGICAL STRATEGIES

Flipped Classrooms

A flipped (or inverted) lesson is one that reverses the usual practice of
teachers presenting direct or guided information to students in class.
Instead, students watch content presented online out of school. Using
that background, students then discuss and analyze what content was
learned outside of class hours. The format allows time for teachers to
interact with students instead of lecturing content for the first time.
Instructors review key ideas in the classroom and students work in groups
to complete math exercises. When in school, students can work through
any gaps or misunderstandings instead of learning it for the first time
there. Students learn by observing the videos, because students can move
at their own pace, and review what they need when they need (Fulton,
2012).

Through this student-centered environment, students have the opportunity to construct viable arguments and critique the reasoning of others.
Additional Common Core Standards of Practice are incorporated in lessons, such as making sense of problems and persevering in solving them
and reasoning abstractly and quantitatively as there is more time for class
discussion. Student-centered learning, via the flipped classroom model, is
flexible and allows for the observation of multiple solution strategies.

Technology

Instructional computer programs can range from presenting complete
lessons featuring direct instruction, a multitude of games and activities
designed for retention practice, and differentiated word problems to
solve, to name only a few of the applications available. An added benefit is
that these online programs provide immediate feedback and remediation
when the students make an error (Van de Walle & Karp, 2012). The wide
variety of concept-based and procedure-driven computer programs available make it possible for students to work independently, cooperatively

with other students, or with the teacher. These activities also serve to heighten interest and self-efficacy. Teachers should preview any platform or program before implementation in the classroom to make certain they are age and ability appropriate and also relate to the subject matter and learners' needs. (Alon & Fuentes, 1998).

VERBAL PERSUASION

In recent years, research has reported that when teachers provide meaningful feedback to students, achievement is enhanced (Stenger, 2015). Offering students constructive guidance about the ways they are studying, reading, searching for information, or answering questions can be invaluable. Being able to know if one is working toward a correct process and/or solution is effective when learning new concepts and practicing skills.

Feedback helps students make corrections in their work and allows them to understand what additional steps are needed or should be changed. Frequent and accurate feedback can assist in the retention aspect of a students' learning, improve accuracy and help students adjust their solutions.

Research-based recommendations for providing students with the kind of feedback that will contribute to increase motivation, build on existing knowledge, and help students reflect on what they've learned are provided below:

1. *Be as Specific as Possible:*   Take the time to provide learners with information on what exactly students did well and what may still need improvement. Tell the learner what he is doing differently than before (Hattie & Timperley, 2007).

2. *The Sooner the Better.*   Numerous studies indicate that feedback is most effective when it is given immediately, rather than a few days, weeks, or months later. In one study that looked at delayed vs immediate feedback, researchers found that participants who were given immediate feedback showed a significantly larger increase in performance than those who had received delayed feedback (Sun, 2012).

3. *Involve Learners in the Process.*   The importance of involving learners in the process of collecting and analyzing performance-based data cannot be overstated. Students should *be given access to information about their performance*. Students need to know if they actually have mastered the material or not. Findings indicate that students who receive formative assessment perform better on a variety of achievement indicators than their peers do. Experts

agree that the practice of frequent and targeted assessment for learning shows promise in its ability to improve student performance (Hanover Research, 2014).

When students have access to this feedback, they develop an awareness of their learning, and are more easily able to recognize mistakes and eventually develop strategies for tackling weak points themselves. Without feedback, it is harder to comprehend objectives, make corrections, and retain the necessary information.

Verbal or written persuasion, then, can be accomplished and effective through feedback offered to students. The comments should be given in a way that is both time effective and boosts student's confidence in their learning. "Feedback can promote learning if it is received mindfully, but it can inhibit learning if it encourages mindlessness" (Bangert-Drowns, Kulik, & Chen-Lin, 1991, p. 58). Lastly, feedback should be given immediately whenever possible to keep students interested in the result of their work and learning, boost confidence, and create a more helpful testing environment. Teachers should give students feedback as often as possible to let students know where they stand.

Verbal persuasion, enactive mastery and vicarious experiences frame the powerful tools that affect students' productive disposition and the relationship to understanding content, procedures and reasoning, the fundamental building blocks of mathematics achievement. What can teachers do to strengthen students' math self-efficacy? A recent New Zealand study (see Bonne & Johnston, 2016; Bonne & Lawes, 2016) gives eight scenarios that strengthen student self-efficacy in math:

1. Students watch other students solve math problems, and/or explain how it was solved (vicarious experience).
2. Students have strategies when content gets challenging (enactive mastery).
3. Students are cognizant of their learning goals (enactive mastery and vicarious experiences).
4. Teachers give students feedback on how they're doing and what they need to do to reach their goals (verbal persuasion).
5. Teachers mentor students by helping them reflect on the role effort played in their success, and what role lack of effort played in any failure (verbal persuasion).
6. Teachers draw students' attention to specific skills they have mastered (enactive mastery, verbal persuasion, and vicarious experiences).

7. Students are encouraged to set an internal standard by which to evaluate their outcomes, rather than just comparing themselves to peers (enactive mastery and verbal persuasion).

8. Teachers and parents refrain from commiserating with students if the teacher or parent found math hard themselves. Rather, they challenge students to success, tell them they expect them to succeed, and other whatever support they can if needed (verbal persuasion).

SUMMARY

This chapter examined the specific ways self-efficacy affects mathematics students, including the strength of the four sources of self-efficacy, and how to incorporate these sources into common math curriculum. We also provided sample assessment tools to assess your students' self-efficacy and suggestions for timetables for doing so. Lastly, we looked at several common topics and examined how sources of efficacy information can be specifically applied to teaching strategies and Common Core curriculum. We ended by summarizing eight simple, yet important, steps teachers can take to increase a student's sense of self-efficacy in mathematics.

In thinking about your students' levels of self-efficacy, it is easy—and understandable—to concentrate on your curriculum. The process of heightening students' levels of self-efficacy, though, should also have as a goal enabling students to generalize their self-efficacy to other classes, and to real-life situations going forward. Goal setting, attributing success or failure to effort (or lack of effort), and internalizing one's own standards and being able to assess one's progress are critical skills every student should develop to achieve lifelong learning goals and to navigate "life events." Today's elementary and middle school students are expected to be engaged with the workforce through the last half of the 21st century, and probably live into the 22nd century. As the world rapidly changes around them, they will need to be critical thinkers and be adept at change. Having heightened self-efficacy in their ability to learn, change, and adapt will mean the difference between success and frustration/failure as they progress through their formal education, and then on to the world they create.

DISCUSSION QUESTIONS

1. How do your curriculum and teaching strategies affect students' levels of self-efficacy?

2.　What changes can you make to either your content or teaching methods to heighten your students' levels of self-efficacy?

3.　Keeping your specific students in mind, how would you assess their levels of self-efficacy? What specific questions would you ask?

4.　How might you involve your students' parents in this effort?

5.　What are the biggest obstacles you can identify to implement the changes recommended in this chapter?

REFERENCES

Alon, S., & Fuentes, D. (Eds.). *Tablets in K–12 education: Integrated experiences and implications.* Hershey, PA: IGI Global Reference Books.

Bangert-Drowns, R. L., Kulik, J., & Chen-Lin, C. (1991). Effects of frequent classroom testing. *The Journal of Educational Research, 85*(2), 89–99.

Bandura, A. (1986). *Social foundations of thought and action: A social cognitive theory.* Englewood Cliffs, NJ: Prentice-Hall.

Bandura, A. (1997). *Self-efficacy: The exercise of control.* New York, NY: W. H. Freeman and Company.

Bonne, L., & Johnston, M. (2016). Students' beliefs about themselves as mathematics learners. *Thinking Skills and Creativity, 20,* 17–28. Retrieved from http://dx.doi.org/10.1016/j.tsc.2016.02.001

Fulton, K. (2012). Upside down and inside out: Flip your classroom to improve student learning. *Learning & Leading with Technology, 39*(8), 12–17.

Hanover Research. (2014). The impact of formative assessment and learning intentions on student achievement. Retrieved from http://www.hanoverresearch.com/media/The-Impact-of-Formative-Assessment-and-Learning-Intentions-on-Student-Achievement.pdf

Hattie, J., & Timperley, H. (2007). The power of feedback. *Review of Educational Research, 77*(1), 81–112. doi:10.3102/003465430298487

Johnson, D. W., & Johnson, R. T. (1989). *Cooperation and competition: Theory and research.* Edina, MN: Interaction Book Company.

Joyce, M. (2016). Cooperative Learning Strategies, National Council of Teachers of Mathematics. Retrieved from http://joyceh1.blogspot.com

Kilpatrick, J., Swafford, J., & Findell, B. (Eds.). (2001). *Adding it up: Helping children learn mathematics.* Washington, DC: National Academy Press.

Kroesbergen, E. H., & Van Luit, J. E. (2003). Mathematics interventions for children with special educational needs, a meta-Analysis. *Remedial and Special Education, 24*(2), 97–114.

National Governors Association Center for Best Practices & Council of Chief State School Officers (2010). *Common Core State Standards for Mathematics.* Washington, DC: Authors.

Organization for Economic Cooperative Development. (2013). Mathematics self-beliefs and participation in mathematics-related Activities. In *PISA 2012 Results: Ready to learn: Students' engagement, drive and self-beliefs* (Vol. III).

Retrieved from http://www.oecd.org/pisa/keyfindings/PISA2012-Vol3-Chap4.pdf

Rivera, D. P. (1996). The University of Texas at Austin, LD Forum: Council for Learning Disabilities. Retrieved from http://www.ldonline.org/article/5932/

Salomon, G., & Globerson, T. (1987). Skills may not be enough: The role of mindfulness in learning and transfer. *International Journal of Educational Research, 11*(6), 623–637.

Schunk, D. H. (1985). Self-efficacy and classroom learning. *Psychology in the Schools, 22*(2), 208–223.

Sharan Y., & Shulov. A. (1989). Cooperative learning, motivation to learn and academic achievement. In S. Sharan (Ed.), *Cooperative learning, theory and research* (pp. 173–202). New York, NY: Praeger.

Stenger, M. (2014). 5 research-based tips for providing students with meaningful feedback. Retrieved from https://www.edutopia.org/blog/tips-providing-students-meaningful-feedback-marianne-stenger

Sun, R. (2012). Instant feedback to help students master math. Retrieved from Howtolearn.com

Van de Walle, J., & Karp, K. S. (2012). *Elementary and middle school mathematics: Teaching developmentally* (8th ed.). Upper Saddle River, NJ: Pearson Education.

Zacharos, K., & Chassapis, D. (2012). Teaching suggestions for the measurement of area in elementary school. Measurement tools and measurement strategies. *Review of Science, Mathematics and ICT Education, 6*(2). Retrieved from http://resmicte.lis.upatras.gr/index.php/review/article/view/1627

CHAPTER 4

ATTENDING
TO PROFESSIONALISM

Addressing the Teacher's Own
Self-Efficacy in Teaching Mathematics

As we have seen in previous chapters, Bandura's (1977, 1997) self-efficacy theory offers explanations for differences observed in the amount of effort students expend in learning new subjects. Students form belief systems in which they believe that they can, or cannot, complete requested mathematical operations. These beliefs are typically formed based on their prior experiences, feedback given from significant others (e.g., parents, teachers), observing the success or failure of peers, and how well they have performed vis-à-vis their internalized goals.

Teachers are not exempt from these psychological traits. Novice as well as seasoned teachers must also grapple with issues of competence, confidence, stress, burnout, and their belief that they can reach even the most difficult student, and help them achieve their mutual academic goals. What does a teacher's sense of self-efficacy look like—and what does it mean? How and when is it formed? What ramifications does a teacher's level of self-efficacy have on student learning? How does a teacher reflect on, and assess, their own level of self-efficacy? Once assessed, how do teachers raise their own levels? How do teachers' perceptions of self-efficacy affect the collective efficacy levels of their colleagues, and vice versa?

Learning Mathematics Successfully: Raising Self-Efficacy in Students, Teachers, and Parents
pp. 71–106

Lastly, what are constructive ways teachers can deal with parents to communicate about their student's level of self-efficacy and ways to elicit their support for understanding and developing mathematical proficiency?

Recall from Chapter 1 the middle school math teacher, Ms. Johnson. She had started her career idealistically believing that her enthusiasm for mathematics would spread to her students. She developed lesson plans with gusto, and looked forward to the challenges that each new school year brought. Ten years on, however, she looked forward more to holiday and summer breaks than to the start of another year. In periods of reflection, she wondered whether she was really reaching students, instilling in them a desire to learn, along with a curiosity about the elegance of mathematical principles? Was she providing them with coping and problem-solving skills that would generalize to new situations? Or, was she going through "the routine" of satisfying district-mandated curriculum based on state and national "standards?" These questions haunted her as she wondered whether or not she really could reach every student and help them succeed, like she believed she would when she began teaching. Were her self-efficacy levels changing, or was she the victim of environmental constraints and operating in a system of lowered building efficacy? How could this be reversed so that she felt positive about her ability to reach students and engender in them her enthusiasm for math?

TEACHER SELF-EFFICACY

Was is teacher self-efficacy? Teacher self-efficacy can be briefly defined as "a teacher's expectation that he or she will be able to bring about student learning" (Ross & Bruce, 2007a, p. 50). While this definition is elegant in its simplicity, it is packed with meaning and underlying assumptions that call for elaboration and study. Indeed, how teachers can best "bring about student learning" through teacher self-efficacy has been the subject of intense scholarly investigation for nearly 50 years. Numerous researchers today anchor their definitions back to Bandura's (1977, 1997) theory that self-efficacy is one's perception of their ability to perform a specific behavior. Since teachers engage in a myriad of "specific behaviors" throughout the school day, the study of teacher self-efficacy is necessarily complex and multidimensional. In order to sift through these behaviors, and make sense of the research findings, we must break down "teacher self-efficacy" into manageable parts. Once we do that, we must address the important "So what?" question—why is this important—important to both teachers and students? How is it measured? Can it be changed, and if so, how? But, before jumping ahead to what it means, operationally, let's review the component parts of self-efficacy theory as it relates to teachers.

Recall from Chapter 1 that all of us—students, faculty, administrators, and parents—operate in environments in which our thoughts and beliefs impact our behavior and environment. The latter, in turn, reflects upon and further informs our thoughts and beliefs (Bandura, 1977). Without necessarily being consciously aware of it, many teachers construct a lesson based on their competence, pacing guides, students' abilities, and what learning objectives they want the class to accomplish. After the lesson is conducted (the behavior), the teacher receives feedback in the form of questions, through nonverbal observations of attentiveness and/or by assessing the extent to which the lesson was successful (the environment). This, in turn, informs teachers as to whether they had perceived both the lesson and outcome accurately and, if not, what changes need to occur to bring about the desired outcomes.

Teacher self-efficacy, then, is the *perception* of one's ability to successfully perform the requisite set of behaviors in order to achieve the desired outcome. Note that two components are present: I can perform the behaviors and, if I do, a desired outcome will occur. For example, our teacher, Ms. Johnson, is developing a unit on adding fractions. Below are some common steps she might take in developing the unit. The questions in parentheses are the questions she is asking herself, consciously or unconsciously, that are assessing her level of self-efficacy with this assignment.

- Do I understand how to add fractions myself? *(How well do I know fractions?)*
- Can I build the content sequentially so that I build on the students' previous knowledge of numbers? *(Do I know where my students are and can I figure out the sequence?)*
- What visuals, or manipulatives, am I going to use to demonstrate the principles of adding fractions? *(Do I know which manipulatives one uses to demonstrate adding fractions, and do I have access to them? If not, can I create my own?)*
- Do I know the time necessary to teach the lesson? *(Do I know how to present the material effectively in the time allowed?)*
- How will I know if the students understand how to add fractions? *(Do I know how to either construct an appropriate assessment and conduct observations that demonstrates students understand, and can perform the skills?)*
- Am I prepared for questions? *(Am I familiar enough with the content so that I can field any question, and explain the content in various ways?)*

- What is the learning objective of this unit? *(What outcome am I look-ing for? How will I know when I have achieved it?)*

As you can see by this example, Ms. Johnson is making judgments throughout the lesson. A highly efficacious teacher will plan the lesson, understand the mathematics content, select the appropriate teaching strategies to teach developmentally, feel confident about fielding ques-tions and addressing confusion, and will effectively assess the lesson out-comes. On the other hand, low efficacious teachers may feel unsure about the content, hope that students do not ask questions that are too difficult, and even be unsure about students' success. Efficacious teachers strive to reach each student, and have strategies in place to bring along those hav-ing difficulty grasping the content. Low efficacious teachers will approach the unit believing that "some will get it, some won't" and believing that no matter what they do, some students simply will not "get it," either because they cannot get it, or do not want to. Highly efficacious teachers will brainstorm with their colleagues, or do a literature search, on effective strategies for teaching difficult content (or difficult students). They believe they can employ a variety of methods to accomplish their goal of students learning the material. Low efficacious teachers tend not to expend this effort. They tend to believe that they either cannot (or prefer not to) master a new method, or that their colleagues likely do not have any useful ideas, or that some students would not grasp the material regardless how much effort the teacher expends.

It is important to remember that self-efficacy has to do with *perceptions* of ability, not necessarily *actual* abilities (Tschannen-Moran, Hoy, & Hoy, 1998). This distinction is important because people can over- or underes-timate their abilities, especially in new situations (e.g., adopting a new teaching method or teaching a new subject) (Hickman, 1993). In some cases, having an inflated perception of one's abilities can be detrimental, such as a teenager driving on snow or ice for the first time and misjudg-ing their abilities, or novice pilots believing they can fly through fog with-out instruments and little experience. In these cases, underestimating one's abilities and acting overly cautiously is prudent and the safer course of action. However, for students and teachers in a traditional learning environment, overestimating abilities can frequently be more beneficial that underestimating them (Bouffard-Bouchard, Parent, & Larivee (1991) because overestimating can lead to actually attempting new behaviors that lead to success. Even if success is not achieved, or is only partially achieved, feedback is obtained that leads to refined behaviors leading to the desired outcomes. Underestimating abilities can easily lead to a belief that failure is imminent thereby negating any desire to even try.

Thus, teachers' self-efficacy is the perception of their ability to perform a specific behavior that leads to a desired outcome (Bandura, 1997). It underlies a teacher's motivation to act (or not), and is affected by whether or not the action leads to an important instructional outcome. It is teachers' self-efficacy that ultimately determines how much effort is expended on lessons and student outcomes. It also predicts how much a teacher will stay current with professional research, and contribute to their departments and building climate. External to the school, a teacher's self-efficacy will determine whether, and how effectively, they interact with parents. Ultimately, it determines whether a teacher burns out, or remains happy and fulfilled in their position.

We examine the ramifications of the teachers' level of self-efficacy on themselves and their students; how self-efficacy is measured; and challenges to raising it for classroom instructors.

How is self-efficacy important to teachers? There is an old adage in medicine of "physician, heal thyself." The underlying message of this phrase, of course, is that a physician cannot help patients if physicians are not taking care of themselves. The same principle holds true of teachers. As educators, we want our students to learn, thrive, and master the content we teach. We want to be the mediators of enhanced student-efficacy. Yet, this can be difficult or impossible if we have not tended to our own self-efficacy and taken steps to insure we are operating at the highest level of self-efficacy possible. Teachers' sense of their instructional self-efficacy has a dual ramification. It affects both student achievement, and teachers' own perceptions, impacting their enthusiasm to teach, motivation to grow and adapt professionally, and ultimately whether a teacher burns out and leaves the profession. This section discusses, separately, these ramifications.

Teacher's Self-Efficacy's Impact on Student Self-Efficacy and Student Achievement. When Bandura first proposed his self-efficacy theory in 1977, it did not take long for educational psychologists, and academics charged with teacher preparation programs, to begin asking whether this psychological theory had direct applications to teachers and students. Issues such as the following arose:

- Could this theory explain why some students persisted in the face of failures and other obstacles, and some did not?
- Could student behavior be changed by heightening self-efficacy through mastery experiences and verbal persuasion?
- Was the same principle operating in the teachers themselves?
- How did the reciprocal relationship between teacher and student affect each other's levels of self-efficacy?

- Does a teacher's level of self-efficacy affect student achievement itself?

In the last 40 years, numerous researchers have tackled these important questions, and have provided considerable evidence that now informs methodology curricula in teacher education programs as well as opportunities for effective professional development (Midgley, Feldlaufer, & Eccles, 1989; Tschannen-Moran et al., 1998; Zee & Koomen, 2016).

Teacher Self-Efficacy Versus Student Self-Efficacy.   One important question is the effect of a teacher's level of self-efficacy on their students' levels of self-efficacy. Over the last several decades, the field has been rife with scholarly studies addressing this question (see, as examples, Hamre & Pianta, 2010; Henson, 2002; Hoy & Woolfolk, 1993, Labone, 2004; O'Neill & Stephenson, 2011; Thoonen, Sleegers, Peetsma, & Oort, 2011). Midgley et al. (1989) studied these effects in a landmark study comparing students' levels of self-efficacy in mathematics as they made the critical transition from elementary school to middle school. Researchers found a positive correlation between students and their elementary school teachers with higher self-efficacy levels. Similar correlations among students of teachers scoring lower on teacher efficacy scales were reported. However, after the transition to middle school, the students' levels of self-efficacy dropped across the board, regardless of gender, background, and previous math abilities. The change may occur as students adjust to a class structure different from elementary school. Despite this initial drop, by the spring semester, high efficacious students with middle school teachers scoring high on teacher efficacy scales had rebounded to their previous efficacy levels, while students entering middle school with low levels who were paired with high-level teachers saw their efficacy levels rise as well. Students with entering low levels paired with low efficacious teachers continued to have low self-efficacy, while students entering with high self-efficacy levels paired with low efficacy teachers tended to recover and regain their usual high efficacy levels. This also suggests that students who have naturally high levels of self-efficacy can be resilient to low efficacious teachers. This also implies that changing students' self-efficacy can be gradual over a semester or two when transferring between elementary and middle school.

Siegle and McCoach (2007) conducted a large randomized pre- and posttest design on nearly 900 fifth grade students in which teachers deliberately tried to raise their students' levels of self-efficacy in mathematics by employing specific strategies gleaned from a professional development workshop designed for that purpose. As teachers' levels of self-efficacy raised during training, they were able to employ specific strategies to then raise their students' levels. The effect size for the treatment was a significant .50 standard deviation units, and this heightened level of efficacy achieved significantly greater achievement in mathematics by the end of the course.

Woolfolk, Rosoff, and Hoy (1990) studied the effects of teacher self-efficacy on students by looking at general attitudes of students toward school and learning between those having high efficacious teachers versus low efficacious teachers. They found that, beyond classroom achievement, those students experiencing high efficacious teachers tended to view school more favorably, viewed learning as interesting and important, and voiced stronger positive evaluations of the teacher.

What these studies suggest is that teachers play an important role in their students' levels of self-efficacy and that a teacher's level of self-efficacy correlates with their students'. All teachers create a classroom climate, or ecology (Tschannen-Moran et al, 1998). Teachers with high levels of self-efficacy create a climate that is welcoming, open, and accepting of prior knowledge. Excitement in finding out new things is heightened, and students are grouped by their abilities to maximum the attention needed to succeed. Curriculum is broken down into manageable chucks designed for students to successfully complete, enabling mastery. Encouragement is provided often, as well as praise for learned skills. Students are guided to attribute success to their hard work, planning, skill and goals, as opposed to "this is your lucky day." For some teachers, this comes naturally. Other teachers, though, are caught in a building or district culture that is very different, suffering from low collective efficacy that dampens the spirit and enthusiasm of individual teachers. Later on in this chapter, we will cover methods of measuring teacher efficacy, strategies to heighten it, and examine how departments and buildings possess a "collective efficacy" that directly affects a teacher and his or her self of personal efficacy.

Teacher Self-Efficacy and Student Achievement.   We have discussed how teacher self-efficacy affects student self-efficacy, and how student self-efficacy affects achievement. But, does teacher self-efficacy directly affect student achievement itself? The primary purpose of education is achievement—the successful acquisition of knowledge in order to build on the acquired knowledge, skills and abilities through subsequent grades with increasingly harder, and more complex, subjects. Without some form of documented "achievement," teachers and administrators would find it difficult to label their school a "success." It is nearly impossible to interest teachers or administrators in theories or practices that do not directly or indirectly affect student achievement itself. Many researchers have investigated the link between a teacher's level of self-efficacy and what their students are able to accomplish. What would account for this link, and what does the teacher self-efficacy/student achievement model look like, operationally?

Tying teacher self-efficacy to student achievement has been the subject of numerous empirical studies across disciplines. Allinder (1995), Hines (2008), Midgley et al. (1989), and Throndsen and Turmo (2013) all found positive correlations between a teacher's level of self-efficacy and heightened student achievement in math, compared to teacher's possessing lower levels of self-efficacy. Moore and Esselman (1992) found that students in the second and fifth grades who had teachers with a greater sense of self-efficacy outperformed their peers in math on the Iowa Test of Basic Skills. Ross (1992) found significantly higher levels of student achievement, as measured by the Ontario Assessment Instrument Pool, among those students of high efficacious versus low efficacious teachers. Watson (1991) found that higher teacher self-efficacy was related to higher math scores across student demographics—in predominately urban, suburban and rural schools.

Significant correlations between teacher self-efficacy and overall student achievement were found in the elementary, middle and high school contexts. In the elementary school, Academic Optimism (a variable closely associated with teacher self-efficacy) was strongly related to student achievement scores in two studies by Chang (2011) and Woolfolk Hoy, Hoy, and Kurz (2008). Chong, Klassen, Huan, Wong, and Kates (2010) and Jimmieson, Hannam, and Yeo (2010) found that perceived academic achievement and climate were positively correlated in middle school. Similar findings were also found in high school, suggesting that students of teachers possessing higher levels of self-efficacy gained higher academic achievement than those of teachers with lower efficacy scores (Caprara, Barbaranelli, Steca, & Malone, 2006; Hardré, Crowson, Debacker, & White, 2006; Mohamadi & Asadzadeh, 2011; Mojavezi & Poodineh Tamiz, 2012).

Despite these consistent findings of high correlations between teachers' levels of self-efficacy and student achievement, we should not interpret these findings as the panacea for addressing all issues of student achievement. Much research needs to refine the exact relationship between teacher efficacy and student achievement, including additional studies that control for other variables associated with achievement (Caprara, et al., 2006).

As well, correlations between variables (in this case, teacher self-efficacy and student achievement) do not prove cause and effect. It merely means there is a *relationship* between the variables, without implied causality. It could be, for example, that students of high ability and motivation serve to reinforce a teacher's perception of his or her effectiveness in teaching. And/or, it could also be that teachers with high efficacy not only reinforce high achieving and motivated students, but increase the achievement and motivation of lower performing students as well. Indeed, such a *quid pro quo* system of reinforcement between students and teachers would be consistent with Bandura's model of triadic reciprocal causation in which teacher behavior, self-efficacy, and student response (e.g., high achievement) affect each other reciprocally (Zee & Kooman, 2016).

What traits or behaviors, then, do teachers with high self-efficacy consistently display that would account for greater student achievement? That is, how does a teacher operationalize his or her self-efficacy in the classroom to maximize student learning? We know that teachers with high self-efficacy believe that they can reach the most difficult student, and have resources in their teaching arsenal to overcome obstacles and other difficulties (Bandura, 1997). But, how do highly efficacious teachers differ from those with lower self-efficacy? Table 4.1 illustrates differences between high and low self-efficacy teachers when it comes to common classroom practices and administrative traits.

Notice that the High Self-Efficacy Traits are really a list of "best practices" for teachers and administrators. Taken at face value, it is not difficult to see how these traits would lead to higher student achievement if only because they create an optimal climate for learning and teacher satisfaction. Yet, student achievement is more difficult to achieve than instrumenting optimal conditions and a happy faculty. Whereas studies report the characteristics of highly efficacious teachers and schools, bringing these conditions about takes work and dedication, as well as a plan and administrative support. For teachers (or schools) with low self-efficacy, it takes a conscious decision to change. The price of not addressing an issue of low self-efficacy may be teacher burnout.

Teacher Self-Efficacy and Burnout.   Systematic study of teacher burnout began in the 1980s when Maslach and Jackson (1981) identified three primary constructs. Attributes particular to this phenomenon are: (1) depersonalization; (2) a feeling of reduced personal accomplishment; and (3) emotional exhaustion. Depersonalization is usually characterized as consciously or unconsciously distancing oneself from other people, whether they be colleagues or students. There can be an emotional detachment in which a teacher no longer really cares what other teachers are doing, nor their successes, nor new skills they might have learned that could help them in their own classroom, nor their personal lives. Depersonalization also occurs when a teacher creates an emotional distance from students, such that all students become faceless "clients" that need to be "taught." These teachers view their classes as a homogeneous group to be accommodated as a "whole."

Burned out teachers lose the ability to take satisfaction and pride in personal accomplishments. Having students succeed in a project is

**Table 4.1.   Differences in Classroom Practices
That Affect Student Achievement**

Area	High Self-Efficacy Traits	Low Self-Efficacy Traits
Teaching strategies	• Believing I can reach every student	• Believing that some students cannot learn/pass
	• Diverse instruction	• Homogeneous instruction aiming for the middle of the road
	• Differentiate instruction frequently	• Same instruction for all students
	• Change goals to meet students' needs	• There is a set goal: to complete the unit
	• Seeks out and learns new instructional methods to help convey the content to struggling students; a lifelong learner	• Uses consistent content from class to class and year to year. Resists new approaches as inadequate and asks for unreasonable "proof" of effectiveness before trying
	• Sees failures as something to work on, and obstacles as something to work around to overcome	• Sees failures and obstacles as confirmation that change is not good and to stop trying
	• Values input from colleagues and seeks out advice and collaborative activities	• Places little value in collegial support, and prefers to work in isolation, teaching things their way— the way they have always been though
Administrative issues	• Administrators are responsive to teacher concerns	• Administrators are either unresponsive to concerns, or unaware of them
	• Administrators encourage trying new ideas	• Administrators resist teachers trying new ideas and punish those who do
	• Encourages democratic participation in departmental and building policies; actively solicits input on how to maximize student learning	• Engages in a top-down management style, with focus more on rules and tradition than student achievement

considered a reason not to complain, as opposed to a reason for joy and satisfaction. Teachers may wonder if they are accomplishing *anything*, let alone anything worthwhile. They consciously wonder "Am I really making a difference? I don't see it."

Emotional exhaustion is the third hallmark sign of burnout. This feeling is more than feeling tired after a long day, or "wiped out" after a tense department meeting or awkward parent conference. It is a chronic exhaustion stemming from a workload that is too heavy, an unusually large number of students needing attention, a difficult or unsupportive administration, or unrealistic expectations by stakeholders such as Boards of Educations, political entities, or the community at large.

Possessing these burnout traits can present themselves in subtle (and not so subtle) teacher-behaviors. Teachers experiencing burnout will gradually withdraw from collegial supports, such as social events in the teacher's lounge, offering ideas at faculty meetings, seeking out colleagues for new ideas and strategies, and taking a personal interest in fellow teachers. They will also distance themselves from students, and withdraw from extracurricular activities whenever possible. While they may have the manners to say socially appropriate things to students in difficult situations (e.g., "I'm sorry your parent died"), they have stopped caring and lump students together as "problem kids" and the "okay ones." Their patience with childhood and adolescence behavior grows thin, and disciplinary referrals increase. Students and colleagues view them as "often irritable." Emotionally, burned out teachers will say "I can't give anymore" "I'm done," or "I don't know what else I can do." Underneath these sentiments are usually uncontrolled stress and anxiety, stemming from a number of possible factors, including an inordinate workload, an unusually difficult set of students, a demanding principal, mandated curriculum viewed as unrealistic, time demands that have grown to impinge on personal time and reflection, family problems, and on and on. The resulting stress and anxiety jade the teacher into questioning their ability to handle students, their ability to successfully teach—let alone adopt new and innovative teaching methods, their value and worth as a colleague, and whether or not they even belong in the profession at all (Tschannen-Moran et al., 1998).

It is important to point out that when thinking about teacher burnout, these traits of exhaustion, depersonalization, and lack of personal accomplishment do not develop suddenly. All teachers (indeed all employees, regardless of their field) experience episodes of exhaustion, and occasional feelings of personal inadequacy. But, these episodes are usually situational and resolve after an immediate crisis has passed, or after a long weekend or break. Teachers experiencing burnout, though, do not "bounce back" after these breaks, and tend to look forward to the resumption of classes with either panic or dread, not excitement and enthusiasm.

One critical aspect of understanding teachers' psychological well-being is to understand the connection between their sense of self-efficacy and their reported level of burnout (Zee & Koomen, 2016). There is a growing interest in teacher burnout and the implication of self-efficacy (Savas, Bozgeyik, & Eser, 2014). Theoretically, we would expect such a relationship to exist and that the relationship would be negative—the higher the level of self-efficacy, the lower the level of burnout. This would be consistent with both self-efficacy and social learning theory's contention that those possessing high levels of self-efficacy would have beliefs of adequacy, as well as the ability to solve problems as they arose. These self-efficacy traits would therefore lead to a reduction of stress and, by extension, a reduction of burnout.

Over the last 20 years, researchers have found strong evidence of this connection, and found it across demographically diverse schools, across international borders, and among levels of teacher experience (Zee & Koomen, 2016). They have also found strong connections with latent variables of burnout, such as perceived stress, job satisfaction, teacher commitment, teacher attrition and retention. For example, teachers registering higher levels of self-efficacy reported significantly lower levels of overall job stress (Barouch Gibert, Adesopea, & Schroeder, 2013), and specifically stress about such things as students' levels of motivation and teaching mixed-ability students. Avanzi, Miglioretti, Velasco, and Balduci (2013) and Salanova, Llorens, and Schaufeli (2011) have conducted longitudinal studies that posit a causal relationship between high levels of self-efficacy and teacher job satisfaction. These findings have been consistently found among elementary faculty (e.g., Collie, Shapka, & Perry, 2012) and middle and high school faculties (e.g., Caprara et al., 2006), and even when assessing all grade levels simultaneously (e.g., Avanzi, 2012; Collie et al., 2012). Regarding attrition and retention, Klassen and Chiu (2011) found that teachers with poor efficacy for classroom management as well as inadequate instructional strategies tended to feel more stress and anxiety about teaching, leading to emotional exhaustion and feeling uncommitted to the profession. In fact, low self-efficacy for classroom management appears to be the most important trigger for leaving their job for both preservice as well as inservice teachers (Canrinus, Helms-Lorenz, Beijaart, Buitnik, & Hofman, 2012).

While researchers find strong correlations between low levels of self-efficacy and unhealthy psychological traits in teachers such as stress and burnout, questions arise as to the direction of causality between self-efficacy and burnout. Do the factors comprising low self-efficacy, such as feelings of inadequacy in reaching students and instructing content, as well as an inability to problem solve and feel confident in meeting the daily challenges teacher face create conditions ripe for burnout? Or, does an accumulation of stress, life-challenges, difficult students, and unreasonable expectations break down even the strongest teacher's sense of self-efficacy? Emerging empirical evidence suggests that the direction of causality is that heightened self-efficacy ameliorates burnout, burnout tends not to decrease high self-efficacy. A recent study by Schwarzer and Hallum (2008) specifically addressed this question in a longitudinal study of 458 teachers. Researchers found a highly significant correlational path between lowered self-efficacy and burnout, whereas no correlation was found on the hypothetical path of burnout leading to lowered self-efficacy. This finding was mirrored by a similar study of 163 randomly chosen German and Syrian teachers conducted by Savas et al. (2014) which found that high self-efficacy was negatively correlated with burn-out, suggesting that those with self-efficacy were more likely to be immune to conditions spawning burnout. Given the large numbers of teachers leaving the profession each year, and the apparent pervasiveness of burn-out among teacher ranks, it is incumbent to address this issue. A key to addressing burnout is the teacher's self-efficacy. Changing self-efficacy requires an honest assessment of one's current levels and a commitment to take positive steps to increase it. Clearly it is important for faculty, principals, and school leaders to consider a teacher's level of self-efficacy in light of burnout. Taking steps to decrease their low performance and beliefs and increase self-efficacy may lead to more confidence and empowerment to command their environments.

How Is Self-Efficacy Measured and Changed?

Background and the Development of Self-Efficacy Measures.   Measuring self-efficacy has evolved over the last 40 years. Measuring one's self-efficacy should be done using instruments that have been subjected to statistical testing for reliability and validity, as well as judged to be actually measuring *self-efficacy* and not a similar construct such as "motivation," "enthusiasm," "competence," or "locus of control." Briefly describing how researchers began measuring this concept, and how the concept of "self-efficacy" has evolved and been applied to teachers, allows us to more fully appreciate how the process informs us as to our strengths and weaknesses of our teaching effectiveness.

Two evaluative studies by the Rand Corporation in the late 1970s (Armor et al., 1976; Berman, McLaughlin, Bass, Pauly, & Zellman, 1977) marked the beginning of empirical study of the self-efficacy construct in educational research. The Rand Studies, as they came to be called, evaluated teaching in in-service training, and curriculum in various schools in the Los Angeles Unified School District. Among the teacher characteristics studied was a construct called "teacher sense of efficacy," which was defined as "the extent to which the teacher believes he or she has the capacity to produce an effect on the learning of students" (Armor et al., 1976, p. 23).

To assess a teacher's "sense of efficacy," the Rand Studies included two items that teachers scored on a 5-point Likert scale from "*strongly agree*" to "*strongly disagree*": "When it comes right down to it, a teacher really can't do much because most of a student's motivation and performance depends on his or her home environment," and "If I really try hard, I can get through to even the most difficult or unmotivated students" (Armor et al., 1976, p. 73). Combining these two items' scores, Rand reported a statistically significant "sense of efficacy" coefficient, indicating that "teachers' sense of efficacy [was] a powerful explanatory variable; it had major positive effects on the percentage of project goals achieved, improved student performance, teacher change, and continuation of project methods and materials" (Berman et al., 1977, p. xi).

A major concern about the Rand findings was their attempt to extrapolate self-efficacy findings from items that had no face validity in actually measuring the phenomenon in the Banduran sense. For example, the first item lists an unspecified teacher behavior ("... really can't do much") coupled with a specific outcome expectation ("... motivation and performance depends on his or her home environment"). This is clearly an *attribution* measure, not a self-efficacy measure—it measures the extent to which a teacher believes efforts are futile because of external forces ("home environment"), not the extent to which a teacher believes he or she is capable of effecting change through teacher behavior.

The second item also incorporates an unspecified teacher behavior ("... really try hard ...") with an unspecified outcome expectation ("... can get through to ..."). Thus, Rand's operational definition of teacher efficacy appears to be a composite of a global teacher efficacy and a global outcome expectation. This is inconsistent with Bandura's contention that efficacy expectations and outcome expectations are two distinct concepts (Bandura, 1977, 1986), and also inconsistent with Bandura's contention that efficacy is a measurement of *specific* behaviors and outcomes.

In fairness to the Rand Studies, however, it should be noted that they based their "efficacy" measures on the theory of personality formulated by Rotter (1966), which is primarily concerned with *causal* relationships between actions and outcomes and an individual's perception of the locus of the reinforcement—whether the outcome is primarily reinforced internally (e.g., internal motives and personal responsibility) or externally (e.g., what other people think, or external rewards like money or bonuses). This is a different concept from personal efficacy in the Banduran sense. For Bandura, self-efficacy and outcome expectations are separate and distinct, and possession of one may or may not signify possession of the other—regardless of the internal or external nature of the outcome expectancy (Bandura, 1986). When the Rand studies' "efficacy" items are analyzed in relation to Rotter's theory of personality, it is clear that the items conform to Rotter's style of assessing internal and external control. Hence, the Rand items are *not* assessing "efficacy," in the sense that efficacy is commonly accepted today.

Initially, some researchers adopted these two Rand "sense of efficacy" items just described in their research on self-efficacy in education. For example, Gusky (1981), Rose and Medway (1981), Ashton (1985), Ashton, Olejnik, Crocker, and McAuliffe (1982) all developed measurement scales that tried to correlate teacher effectiveness with Rotter's underlying theory of control by asking variations of the two Rand studies items discussed above. While these studies and instruments did not become the standard for measuring self-efficacy, they did provide an important basis for educational researchers to begin examining these constructs, and applying psychometric testing to determine what, exactly, was being measured and its statistical significance.

By the early to middle 1980s, a second strand of inquiry was emerging based more on Bandura's theory of self-efficacy. The commonly used Gibson and Dembo's Self-Efficacy Scale (1984) consisted of 30 items on an 8-point Likert scale of *strongly disagree* to *strongly agree*. Sample questions include "When a student does better than usual, many times it is because I exerted a little extra effort," and "If a teacher has adequate skills and motivation, she/he can get through to the most difficult students." When the 30-item instrument was factor analyzed, however, Gibson and Dembo were surprised to find two related, but distinct, factors. The first factor was labeled personal teaching efficacy and was assumed to be related to Bandura's concept of self-efficacy. The second factor was labeled just "teaching efficacy" and later relabeled "general teaching efficacy" assuming that it captured the second part of social learning theory: Outcome expectancy (Gibson & Dembo, 1984).

Examples of "personal teaching efficacy" included:

- "If a student mastered a new math concept quickly, this might be because I knew the necessary steps in teaching that concept.
- "When the grades of my students improve it is usually because I found more effective teaching approaches.
- "When I really try, I can get through to [the] most difficult students.
- "If a student does not remember information I gave in the previous lesson, I would know how to increase his/her retention in the next lesson."

Examples of "general teaching efficacy" included:

- "A teacher is very limited in what he/she can achieve because a student's home environment is a large influence on his/her achievement.
- "If students are not disciplined at home, they aren't likely to accept any discipline.

- "The hours in my class have little influence on students compared to the influence of their home environment.
- "The amount that a student can learn is primarily related to family background."

While other researchers testing Gibson and Dembo's landmark instrument also identified two distinct factors, continued research identified inconsistencies on which factors some items loaded, and additional psychometric testing questioned what constructs, exactly, the instrument was measuring (Tschannen-Moran & Hoy, 2001). This lack of statistical and conceptual clarity was problematic on two fronts. First, in order to refine self-efficacy theory as it related to teachers and students, researchers needed instruments that were conceptually sound in measuring that which they purported to measure. Second, instrumentation used in professional development experiences for teachers needed to carry sufficient confidence that scores on these instruments accurately reflected meaningful measurements of a teacher's attitudes toward teaching and their students.[1]

Bandura (1997) cautioned educators that teacher self-efficacy was not uniform across the many tasks and functions a teacher was asked to perform, nor was it uniform across subject matter. For example, a teacher could feel very efficacious about dealing with parents about a child's progress, but not as efficacious dealing with classroom management. A math teacher could also feel efficacious about teaching middle school fractions, but less confident about algebraic equations. He responded by circulating a 30-item instrument containing seven subscales: efficacy to influence decision making; efficacy to influence school resources; instructional efficacy; disciplinary efficacy; efficacy to enlist parental involvement; efficacy to enlist community involvement; and efficacy to create a positive school climate (Tschannen-Moran & Hoy, 2001).

While no reliability nor validity information has ever been published on this instrument (Tschannen-Moran & Hoy, 2001), it did focus researchers on the importance of providing enough specificity in items to measure specific teacher functions and behavior without becoming too narrowly focused. As Tschannen-Moran and Hoy aptly described it,

This is a danger of developing measures that are so specific they lose their predictive power for anything beyond the specific skills and contexts being measured (e.g., I am confident I can teach simple subtraction to middle-income second graders in a rural setting who do not have specific learning disabilities, as long as my class is smaller than 22 students and good manipulatives are available. (2001, p. 795)

Deciding the level of specificity needed to assess a teacher's self-efficacy often depends on the purposes of the assessment, such as, for academic and scholarly research purposes, or for a teacher's personal use, or as part of a department or building professional development exercise. This distinction is critically important for teachers and administrators to make, especially when choosing an instrument to use in professional development, or even preservice education. Since the audience of this book is preservice teacher candidates, and in-service teachers in professional development settings, our focus will be on assessment in those contexts, as opposed to inordinate attention to psychometric testing of instruments used in reliability and validity studies. Indeed, when even Bandura's instrument was field-tested among real-world teachers, the teachers determined that 7 of the 30 items did not really represent their work. Items such as "How much can you influence the class size of your school?" "How much can you do to get businesses involved in your community?" and "How much can you do to get churches involved in working with your school?" were deemed as not very important, nor central, to their work in three studies conducted by Tshannen-Moran and Hoy (2001) in the early 2000s.

Determined to address both the conceptual and statistical issues raised by earlier researchers that occurred during the last 3 decades of the 20th century, Tshannen-Moran and Hoy (2001) developed the Ohio State Teacher Efficacy Scale, later renamed simply Teachers' Sense of Efficacy Scale. Through several iterations over three studies with real-life preservice and in-service teachers, a 24-item instrument is scored on a 9-point Likert scale with values ranging from *not at all* to *a great deal*. Factor analyses revealed three distinct factors embedded in the scale: Efficacy for Instructional Strategies (8 items); Efficacy for Classroom Management (8 items); and Efficacy for Student Engagement (8 items) accounting for a respectable 54% of variance. The long form (24 items) and shorter form (12 items), along with reliability data and scoring instructions of this Teacher Efficacy Scale is contained in Appendix A of this book.

Of all the instruments examined in researching this book, this instrument satisfies the most requirements for practical administration as well as demonstrated reliability and validity testing of any examined. This instrument can be used individually by a teacher to assess his or her own level of self-efficacy. A scoring guide (see Appendix A) allows a teacher to assess a composite score on each of the three identified factors of Instructional Strategies, Classroom Management, and Student Engagement. These scores can be obtained over time to assess attitudinal changes based on professional development or just maturity through experience. Second, the instrument can be given to departments, or even buildings, for administrators to get an assessment of the faculty's levels that could inform principals or superintendents (and the faculty themselves) on areas needing attention. Because these are self-report measures, teachers are obviously encouraged to be reflective and honest, but administrators—if administered in a professional development context—would also be wise to think about whether the results they get are congruent with their own observations of the teachers' efficacies. Forms like this, because they are self-report and because they are used for professional development, can also be slightly modified, if needed, to incorporate items germane to a specific teacher, or specific building. For example, a teacher (or department or building) may choose to add an item(s) that assess a teacher's self-efficacy in teaching specific content, or addresses idiosyncratic issues like effectively dealing with diverse socioeconomic backgrounds of students, or even unusual community realities. Forms such as the Teacher Efficacy Scale contained in Appendix A provide a comprehensive teacher self-efficacy assessment, but the overarching goal of such instruments is to provide reflective information to the teacher and/or colleagues/administrators for professional development purposes. Thus, care should be taken to make sure that all important areas of specific teachers' activities be assessed to provide the most helpful and comprehensive snapshot possible.

Changing Teacher Self-Efficacy.   Once self-efficacy levels are assessed, we think about what teachers can do to heighten their levels. Are they malleable and, if so, when in a teacher's career are the changes most likely to occur? What specific strategies can teachers and administrators employ through professional development activities to maximize chances of success?

Bandura (1977, 1997) has consistently maintained that self-efficacy beliefs are most malleable during early stages of learning. Regardless of one's level at the outset of a new behavior, whether it be driving, parenting, or teaching, people accumulate and digest information as new skills are tried as to their success at performing these behaviors. If initial attempts are clumsy or unsuccessful, self-efficacy levels can be low, only to rise quickly if initial failure is met with success and mastery. Established efficacy beliefs, such as in seasoned/tenured teachers, are more difficult to change, and requires forceful evidence to dispute the preexisting disbeliefs in one's ability to perform. Bandura (1997) has hypothesized, in fact, that a person will hold their self-efficacy beliefs in a provisional status until they are able to successfully test new skills. These findings have implications in how both teacher preparation and professional development work.

Attention has been focused on changes that occur in teachers' self-efficacy during their early careers when the construct is most malleable. Hoy and Spero (2005), Woolfolk and Hoy (1990), and Tschannen-Moran et al. (1998) all found increases in preservice levels of self-efficacy only to see them significantly decline during the first year of teaching. A variety of reasons may contribute to the change, such as a preservice teacher's underestimating the complexity of what teaching entails, the various agendas that must be accommodated, and generally realizing that teaching is more challenging than applying classroom strategies. This drop during the first year of teaching, if not reversed by eventual success and feeling of competence, can lead to disillusionment so great as to drive the teacher from the profession (Savas et al., 2014). However, beginning teachers who felt they had received constructive feedback, achieved a reasonable level of success, and a building support system (anything from an assigned mentor to friendly colleagues) felt better about their choice of becoming a teacher. These early career instructors given supports felt they were impacting student learning is a positive way, and even had more positive feelings about their teacher preparation programs (Hoy & Spero, 2005).

The implications for teacher preparation programs are profound. The timing of authentic classroom experience and adequate support to teach and assess their students can affect future teachers' immediate and long term career success. Though the support of advisors and the student teacher's cooperating teacher can easily buoy the teacher candidate's self-efficacy during the student teaching semesters, confidence can drop sharply when novice teachers are hired and assigned their own set of classes, as reported by Hoy and Spero (2005) and Woolfolk and Hoy (1990). The investigators also found significant differences in preservice teachers who had a sudden student teaching immersion into teaching as opposed to those who had been introduced into the profession more gradually through classroom internships and other types of in-building experiences. The student teaching-only group exhibited a significantly lower drop in self-efficacy, while those with prior in-building experiences experienced little or no drop.

The College of Education at the University of Missouri-St. Louis developed the Studio School concept to address the issue of providing authentic and effective classroom experiences for all teacher education candidates (see Sherman, Hickman, & Basile, 2015). Teacher candidates observe and work with students during each preparation course leading to the final practicum semesters. During those two semesters, the program placed preservice teachers in groups in area schools, working in a variety of grade levels and/or teachers, depending on the grade levels. Aspiring teachers have experience in instruction, sitting in on parent conferences when appropriate, tutors for small groups of struggling, on-level or excelling students, playground supervision and in any and all roles teachers assume. Preservice teachers report to schools when they open the school year and remain throughout each full semester. In that way, the new teachers experience the activities that schools put in place to open and close an academic year. This immersion into a building's practices and culture enables students to gain invaluable experience by observing a variety of teachers, classes, and issues—over time. Whereas not designed specifically to heighten, or maintain, teacher self-efficacy, this effect has clearly been a positive by-product. While the program is too new for longitudinal data, preliminary and anecdotal data suggest that teachers enter their first year of teaching with a more realistic grounding of the stresses of beginning teaching, a more realistic assessment of their strengths and weaknesses, and more committed to their decision to become a teacher than teachers who graduated prior to this development.

Experienced and tenured teachers demand a different approach to professional development and strategies to heighten their self-efficacy. Change can be difficult, threatening, and time-consuming. Resistance can come in many forms, but a common one is a statement such as "I'm fine with what I'm doing now. I think it works. Why should I change?" Underneath that statement, though, is a psychological process of not being clear what the goals of the change are, if they can successfully perform required behaviors to affect the change, and a firmly held belief that what they are already doing "works"—regardless of whether that is true. If the teacher(s) believe that change is beneficial, and they want professional development in acquiring a new skill(s), great. While that may eliminate resistance to trying, it still requires adequate support and opportunities to successfully master the new skill.

Administrators should consider, when developing professional development activities for teachers to raise their self-efficacy in specific areas (e.g., a new instructional method, classroom management, embellishing the curriculum) what are the *goals* of the requested development? Why is this change being proposed? How will it make [fill in the blank] better? Without specific goals, or a perceived outcome, little effort will be expended to change. Yet, the goals or outcomes themselves will appear useless to teachers if they doubt their ability to master the requested changes (Bandura, 1997).

Planning activities that have, as an ultimate goal, a change in teachers' self-efficacy levels in order to drive an innovation requires thoughtful planning. Having teachers attend a short-term program on an innovation may pique their interest, or perhaps even create a temporary bump in their belief in their ability to do it. However, studies have shown that these bumps in efficacy are transient, usually disappearing within 6 weeks as teachers try something, fail (or not perform as successfully or comfortably as they would like) and revert back to behaviors they are used to and with which they are comfortable (Huber, Fruth, Avila-John, & Lopez-Ramirez,

2016; Ross, 1994; Ross & Bruce, 2007; Savas et al., 2014; Tschannen-Moran et al., 1998). These researchers have each conducted extensive research on the effectiveness of efficacy training with innovating math teachers' instructional methods. The authors caution against expecting classroom changes without adequate follow up and sensitivities to self-efficacy by supporting teachers' opportunities to succeed, and provide encouragement, and feedback.

Recalling Bandura's stated sources of efficacy information informs us of approaches best suited for skill transfer to occur. Here is one approach that could be used that is sensitive to time constraints, yet provides adequate supports to encourage adopting planned innovations.

Step 1: Identification. What innovation is planned (e.g., introducing a new teaching method for teaching algebraic equations, or a new classroom management technique, or changing curriculum and teaching methods to meet new standardized tests)?

Step 2: Goals. Why is this change important? How does it differ from the usual ways of doing things? What evidence exists that the proposed change will lead to the goal? Will the teachers accept that this is a worthwhile goal?

Step 3: Teaching Methods. Will this be a PD workshop day? Who will do it? What materials will be used? Will there be follow up meetings? How will the teacher's current comfort level with the change (self-efficacy) be measured?

Step 4: Transfer. How will the four sources of efficacy be accommodated and incorporated into the planned program?

- Mastery Experiences: What conditions are being planned that allow teachers to practice new skills and refine and perfect the strategies?

- Vicarious Learning: How can teachers observe successful performance of the requested behavior—through demonstration? Through workshops? Observing peers who are proficient?

- Verbal Persuasion: How is a teacher given positive and constructively negative feedback on their attempts to perform the behavior? By whom? How often?

- Physiological States: Is the teacher nervous or upset by the proposed changes? What is planned to focus them on their potential success?

Step 5: Evaluation. What does success look like? Does booster training need to occur? Are the requested changes observable? Do teachers feel comfortable and confident in the requested innovations? If not, what would make them comfortable?

Professional development activities for tenured teachers is more than arranging an afternoon after-school talk on a new innovation. It requires forethought as to the purpose of the change, how teachers are likely to react to it, whether you can convince them of its value and their ability to be successful, and tapping into what we know best enables success: providing mastery experiences, watching others perform it successfully, and verbal encouragement.

Figure 4.1 illustrates a model of teacher change developed by Ross & Bruce (2007) pertaining to professional development of Grade 8 math teachers, and reinforces the steps in effective teacher development outlined above. Central to the process is the *teacher's* own self-assessment about how well they achieved the instructional goals, its effect on student achievement, and their overall satisfaction and comfort with the proposed changes. Peers and "change agents" (in this case, PD) serve to also inform the teacher of their effectiveness, all of which influences the teacher's sense of self-efficacy, whether they persist in adopting the instructional innovation, and how that influences goals they set. Taken as a whole, the teacher then makes an assessment on the impact on student achievement, and makes a judgment as to whether their actions have made a positive difference.

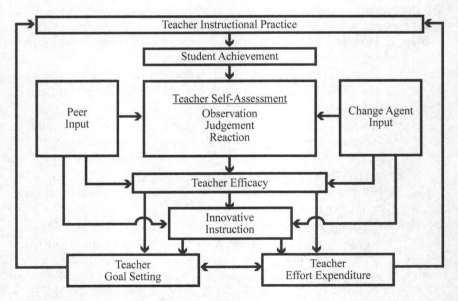

Figure 4.1.   Model of teaching self-assessment as a mechanism for teacher change (Ross & Bruce, 2007b). Used with permission.

COLLECTIVE EFFICACY

As we have seen, teacher efficacy is an important predictor in how much effort and commitment teachers will expend in creating lessons and attending to the educational needs of their students. The attitudes and assumptions of a teacher's colleagues, particularly regarding a building's students' ability to learn and other facets of the educational enterprise, often directly affects individual teachers' sense of their own abilities (Bandura, 1997). Thus, just as we attend to individual teacher's sense of self-efficacy, we must also attend to the cultural norms operating in specific buildings. These norms, or assumptions, by the faculty as a whole constitutes a building's *collective efficacy*. Examining traits of efficacious *buildings* or *departments*, as the faculty of a whole, can inform us of attitudes (and resulting practices) that either reinforce—or impede—student learning. Assessing a faculty's sense of collective efficacy can be easily, and reliably, done. The harder (but not impossible) part is changing it. How does that happen? How long does it take? What does it look like? What evidence exists that such changes can—or should—happen?

We have seen that a teacher's sense of self-efficacy influences a student's sense of self-efficacy and vice versa. This reciprocal relationship often allows a teacher to positively influence students' perceptions of their abilities to succeed in class by believing in their ability, sometimes even before the student does. Conversely, having a class of low-achieving students can adversely affect a teacher's sense of efficacy unless the teacher's efficacy is strong and resilient to the challenge of having a class of underperforming students.

The same principle holds when considering the teacher's beliefs and attitudes, and the beliefs and attitudes of teachers' colleagues (Bandura, 1997). There can be two effects on a school's faculty when a teacher with high self-efficacy is hired in a building of instructors with lower self-efficacy. Either the highly efficacious teacher will pull up the levels of his or her colleagues, or possibly, the teacher will be pressured by cultural norms to adopt the prevailing group beliefs (e.g., our students do not perform well, so don't expect much). If new teachers do not conform, they can be labeled as "naïve" or "idealistic." This incongruence of beliefs among teachers often leads highly efficacious teachers to seek employment elsewhere. This situation can influence the low-efficacious culture to become more cohesive and perpetuates the cycle of failure (Bandura, 1997). However, the reverse can also be true: Teachers who possess low self-efficacy are often positively influenced by those with higher levels. Conforming to the cultural norms of the building, low self-efficacious teachers can adopt more positive and active beliefs regarding their students' abilities (Goddard, Hoy, & Hoy, 2000; Ware & Kitsantas, 2007).

What, then, are the traits of building faculty possessing a sense of high collective efficacy versus low collective efficacy? Teachers possessing high collective efficacy, first and foremost, believe in students' abilities to learn, regardless of their race, gender, or socioeconomic status; they believe in their ability to set realistic achievement goals for students, even if those goals are challenging for the faculty to identify; they exhibit a strong, cohesive, and collegial organizational effort through meetings, professional development and information sharing; they persist when plans fail by reexamining approaches and trying new strategies; and they actively engage parents in conversations about the school's operation, its curriculum and their child's progress (Bandura, 1997; Goddard et al., 2000). Faculties possessing low collective efficacy may not believe as strongly in their students' abilities to learn and may frequently doubt their students and/or their families are motivated to learn. Thus, these teachers expend less effort ("What difference does it make?"), shun professional development in newer methods and ideas ("What I do is good enough"), and give up easily on suggested changes ("I told you it wouldn't work").

Regardless of whether a building has high collective or low collective efficacy, it is easy to see how such beliefs become a self-fulfilling prophecy for students and their achievement. Buildings with high collective efficacy see students excel, and meet teacher and district achievement standards (Bandura, 1997; Brinson & Steiner, 2007; Goddard et al., 2000; Ware & Kitsantas, 2007). This, in turn, reinforces not only specific teacher's sense of self-efficacy, but that of the entire faculty, and spurs them to reach even greater heights of efficacy and excellence to enhance, as much as possible, student achievement. Conversely, students in a building of low collective efficacy will live up to the teachers' expectations too—of low achievement and underperformance, thus reinforcing the teachers' beliefs that these are, in fact, underachieving students who don't care. This perpetuates these teachers' feelings of futility in even trying.

Changing the collective efficacy of buildings with low efficacy is challenging, but not impossible. It must start with principals and district leaders committing to such changes, even if it means restructuring schools and bringing in administrators who are determined to make these changes (Bandura, 1997; Brinson & Steiner, 2007; Goddard et al., 2000; Ware & Kitantas, 2007). Usually, the districts begin with a set of goals that high collective efficacy should achieve. Four common and encompassing goals could be (1) improve student achievement; (2) ameliorate the negative effects of low socioeconomic status; (3) improve parent/teacher relationships; and (4) create a work environment that builds teacher commitment to the school (Brinson & Steiner, 2007). Let us examine each of these goals within the context of collective efficacy, and why it is important to address them when instituting systemic change within the educational organization.

Goal #1: Improve Student Achievement.   Most would agree that the most important function of a school is to educate its students to acquire the knowledge and skills mandated by the district's curriculum. Because of mandated testing standards as a common measure of student achievement, most administrators and teachers ask themselves "how will this affect student achievement?" when presented with new ideas, proposed changes in curriculum, as well as nearly every activity sponsored by the school. This book has provided compelling evidence connecting a teacher's sense of self-efficacy with student achievement. Yet, having a class of students excel in math because the math teacher has high self-efficacy does not necessarily help the school's scholastic record if those students are underperforming in other subjects such as language arts and history. Since collective efficacy is contagious among teachers (Bandura, 1997), striving to elevate the efficacy levels of the faculty body increases the chances of students achieving in all academic areas.

Goal #2: Ameliorate the Negative Effects of Low Socioeconomic Status (SES). Students from low socioeconomic status homes may have parents (or guardians) who are not connected to the school, do not understand the purpose nor strategies of the curriculum, may not value the benefits of education, and may have had bad experiences with school authorities because their prior experiences have been negative—perhaps dealing with discipline issues with their child. Other lower SES children may come from homes whose parents greatly appreciate the value of education, but have few resources to provide extracurricular activities or other enriching experiences that more advantaged children have. These students start their public school career behind more advantaged students, and fall further behind as they progress through grades (Bandura, 1997). These students become perceived by faculty as chronically underperforming, prone to absenteeism and other disciplinary problems. Studies by Bandura (1993) and Goodard et al. (2000) provide empirical evidence that this perception need not be the case. In both studies, students from urban schools achieved academic mastery in reading and mathematics, directly traceable to the collective efficacy of the faculty of their buildings, when factors associated with SES were controlled. Whereas research is continuing on the precise effect of collective efficacy on student achievement, especially in urban districts comprised of students of lower SES, emerging evidence consistently demonstrates that SES need not be an impediment to a student's academic achievement, *if* the teachers of their buildings believe in them, and structure the lessons to meet their needs and create the conditions necessary for their success (Bandura, 1993, 1997).

Goal #3: Improve Parent/Teacher Relationships.   In buildings with low collective efficacy, parent-teacher relationships tend to be minimal, or nonexistent, and may only revolve around problems a student is facing (or causing). If probed, teachers may voice the opinion that their students' parents "don't care" and never show up for parent-teacher conferences. In reality, Ross and Gray (2006) suggest that involving parents carries certain risks for faculty of low collective efficacy. Teachers may not feel confident in defending the school's curriculum or values, or they may be challenged by ideas and values other than their own. Faculty of buildings with high collective efficacy welcome parental involvement, and do not worry about challenges and differing opinions—they are confident in handling these issues and conversations with parents. Indeed, they deliberately reach out to parents to elicit their support of the curriculum, provide concrete ways parents can reinforce the lessons presented, and ask parents for feedback (e.g., "What is your student telling you about their classes—are they happy with school, feel they're learning? Are they struggling?"). Reaching out to parents also enables teachers to become aware of nonschool issues that may be affecting a student's behavior, attitude, or performance, such as a sick relative, divorce, or financial issues facing the family. Teachers from high collective efficacy buildings persist in spite of canceled appointments and nonreturned phone calls and/or emails. Some teachers may even drive to students' residences for a home visit (Bandura, 1997).

Two practical examples of how forming effective connections with parents can benefit children's academic achievement exist in urban districts in St. Louis, Missouri. In the early 2000s, both districts were financially stressed and one had lost full accreditation due to not meeting Missouri standardized assessments and high absenteeism, coupled with an unacceptably low graduation rate. After hiring new superintendents, concerted efforts were made to turn these districts around by staff development and hiring of new key administrators whose goal it was to change the districts' culture—building by building—to enhance collective efficacy. When teachers and administrators reached out to parents, and listened to them, they discovered that many of the low-income students did not attend regularly because they had few clothes and felt conscious about wearing the same thing day after day. Other families had no washer or dryer, leading to being embarrassed by dirty clothes. In the other district, many families did not have adequate food supplies, let alone good nutritional choices. For the district in which clothes were a problem, a "clothes bank" was formed with gently worn donated clothes, and washers and dryers were installed in an unused room, freely available to families or students to use during school hours. In the other district, a food bank was created with fruits and vegetables grown on school property by science classes studying plants (as well as community-donated staples). In both instances, taking care of primary needs of struggling students gave them the respect they needed to at least attend school, and in the other district, to not go hungry. Achievement scores soared, the community passed bond issues that renovated buildings and erased deficits, and the district regained full accreditation. Forming these parental connections directly, and indirectly, led to not only community goodwill (e.g., passage of bond issues), but also helped students satisfy primary needs in order to feel capable of attending class regularly. These types of examples do not represent complicated, nor expensive, investments on a district's part. But, they do require some outside-the-box thinking in terms of how schools can respond to community needs, and interact with parents in new ways. Chapter 5 examines parental self-efficacy, and proposes strategies teachers can use to work with parents regarding their student's academic achievement.

Goal #4: Create a Work Environment That Builds Commitment to the School. Schools with low collective efficacy may have built an environment that builds commitment to neither students nor the organization. Teachers who fit this mold will spend their free period complaining in the teacher's lounge, and expend minimal effort to meet district goals. If they are asked to participate in policy decisionmaking, which is rare, they opt for the easiest goals possible, requiring the least amount of effort on their parts. This would be consistent with a teacher who ultimately believes that those who want to learn will, and those who do not will not, and there is little a teacher can do about it anyway. Teachers who do not fit this mold—the highly efficacious ones—will become frustrated, isolated, and soon leave to find a district or building that more closely shares their passion for learning (Bandura, 1997; Ware & Kitsantas, 2007).

Supporting the work climate change is the responsibility of principals and other district officials who recognize the perils of low collective efficacy and who are committed to turning a building (or district) around to increase teacher efficacy, student efficacy, and ultimately, student achievement (Bandura, 1997; Brinson & Steiner, 2007; Goddard et al., 2000; Protheroe, 2008; Ware & Kitsantas, 2007). What does such an administrative endeavor look like? Who is involved and how does it work?

Brinson and Steiner (2007) provide a case study of a struggling elementary school in Bolingbrook, Illinois that exemplifies effective leadership and faculty dedication to turn a building around. In 2001, a Bolingbrook elementary school was one of the lowest performing schools in the district, with only 57% of students meeting expectations on state tests. In 1997, the principal had organized teachers into "cadres" with the leader serving on the "school leadership team." Although this change improved communication and enhanced shared decisionmaking among faculty and administration, resulting in improved student behavior and school climate, academic performance continued to lag.

In response to this news, the school leadership team and principal went on a 2-day "data retreat" where teachers learned how to analyze student performance so that they could improve their ability to make data-driven instructional decisions. The school leadership team returned and taught these skills to every faculty member in the building. The results were impressive: Testing scores increased every year beginning the following year (2002) and, by 2007, students meeting or exceeding state testing standards had risen to 70%, despite steady increases in the numbers of low-income students and English language learners.

What finally accounted for this increase in student achievement? The researchers trace back the underlying cause to the building's change in collective efficacy. In summarizing their case study, they write:

> In the case of [this elementary school], the teachers believed in some fundamental sense that they could, as a group, significantly improve student learning. It is important to note that, although the supportive and warm relationships that developed among the school leadership team and the cadres appear to have played a vital role in the success of the data retreat intervention, relationships alone were not enough to produce results in student academic performance. Only through focused and ongoing professional development and specific actions on the part of the principal were the teachers of [this elementary school] able to dramatically improve student performance. (p. 1)

Bandura (1997) cautions that systemic change resulting in enhanced collective efficacy rarely comes quickly. In this case study just provided, various methods were tried over 4 years before the new approach (data-driven instructional decision making) started making a difference. Teachers had also been given a voice through shared decisionmaking with administrators, allowing them to "own" both the process and the results. It also demonstrated a tenacity to persist in the face of disappointing results (4 years of lagging test scores), and demonstrated a belief that scores could rise with their population of students. These beliefs and this tenacity are hallmarks of elevated teacher efficacy.

Lastly, this case study effectively operationalized the three strongest influencers of self-efficacy: mastery experiences, vicarious experiences, and verbal persuasion. Just as raising an individual teacher's self-efficacy relies on these influences, raising a faculty's collective efficacy employs the same process. Do teachers have a chance to practice new behaviors safely—and fail? Are there built-in opportunities to learn from other teachers, share experiences, and get feedback? Are principals and other school leaders supportive and offer positive reinforcement? Is ample time given to experiment, get feedback, fail, try again, and work toward feeling comfortable with a new behavior? Developing collective efficacy is about trust, both among a teachers' colleagues and among their administrators, coupled with a belief that all students can learn, given the right environment constructed by the school.

Measurement of Collective Efficacy.   The collective efficacy of a building can be understood by listening to what teachers say, whether it be in casual conversation in the faculty lounge, or during faculty meetings. Indeed, this is frequently the first hint to a sensitive principal that collective efficacy may be low. Apart from this informal and anecdotal method, there are two more reliable measurement possibilities. One is to assess and calculate the total score of teachers' self-efficacy to determine a mean score. This would provide a closer approximation of the building's collective efficacy. The third method is to have every faculty member complete an assessment instrument designed specifically for this purpose. This is the preferred method as collective efficacy may possess subtle variations among a group of teachers that are not neatly reflected in assessments of individual teachers (Bandura, 1997; Goddard et al., 2000).

In examining the literature on collective efficacy, only two instruments were found that had achieved adequate reliability and criterion related validity through rigorous psychometric testing. Each instrument asked similar items found on various teacher self-efficacy forms, but phrased the items along the lines of "we" as opposed to "I." Moreover, these instruments also more closely assessed climate variables, such as perceived support received from principals and school leaders.

 Goddard et al. (2000) published a 21-item Collective Teacher Efficacy Scale that asks such questions as "If a child doesn't learn something the first time, teachers will try another way;" "Teachers in this school are skilled in various methods of teaching;" "Teachers in this school are able to get through to difficult students;" "The quality of school facilities here really facilitates the teaching and learning process;" and "Teachers here don't have the skills needed to produce meaningful student learning." In using this instrument to examine urban elementary schools, collective teacher efficacy was positively associated with student achievement in mathematics and reading.

Ware and Kitsantas (2007) developed a 17-item form consisting of three factors: (1) teacher efficacy to enlist administrative support; (2) teachers' influence on decisionmaking; and (3) teacher efficacy for classroom management. Examples of items include: "The administration's behavior toward the staff is supportive" (administrative support); "The principal talks with me frequently about my instructional practices" (administrative support); "Teachers' views are elicited on issues relating to student discipline" (decisionmaking); "Teachers are involved in establishing curriculum" (decisionmaking); "Teachers determine the amount of homework" (classroom management); and "Teachers are able to select their teaching techniques" (classroom management).

Theoretically, an administrator (or group of teachers) could devise their own form specifically tailored to their building or the specific information for which they are inquiring. While such forms have not been subjected to reliability and validity testing, they can provide pertinent information about a specific building. Generally, though, it is advised to use published instruments that have been subjected to reliability and validity testing to insure faith that the results are meaningful and that collective efficacy of the faculty is actually being measured.

SUMMARY

This chapter examined self-efficacy from the perspective of the teacher, both in terms of their personal teaching self-efficacy as well as the collective efficacy of their colleagues. We examined what self-efficacy is to a teacher, how it is measured, how it is changed, and the important role it plays in student achievement. We examined the psychological constructs underlying self-efficacy, how they grew out of Rotter's theory of internal/external causation, and evolved through Bandura's social-learning and self-efficacy theories.

Self-efficacy is contextual in that levels can vary across the many functions of a teacher's day. Self-efficacy can vary among subjects and grade levels, various class populations, as well as noninstruction based activities. It is not a one-size-fits-all assessment of a teacher's strength. Instead, it is a barometer informing teachers of areas in which they feel especially strong and confident, or areas in which they are unsure or ill-prepared. Knowing these specifics can lead to self-directed professional development tailor-made for maximum effectiveness. Taken as a whole, a teacher's overall level of self-efficacy greatly influences the extent to which he or she is going to affect student achievement by predicting the extent to which they expend extra effort, believe in a student's ability to learn, and persist with a student until success is achieved. Additionally, we examined the malleability of self-efficacy in preservice and induction-year teachers versus tenured teachers. Each group can change and improve their levels of self-efficacy, but seasoned teachers who often hold long-held beliefs can be harder to change. Care must be taken to provide the professional development appropriate for each group, and to couch proposed changes in clearly defined goals to which teachers subscribe.

Self-efficacy is also negatively associated with teacher burnout such that the former tends to insulate teachers from stresses and failures. Teachers and administrators alike must be sensitive to the symptoms of teacher burnout and take steps to reverse it. Ignoring symptoms lead not only to teacher underperformance, but the negative attitudes expressed by teachers can be contagious to other faculty. Moreover, ignoring teacher burnout can lead to unnecessary turnover in areas of critical shortage, such as mathematics education.

Collective efficacy is equally important to the school climate in terms of being welcoming and accepting, and adjustable to individual needs, or rigid and laden with rules and protocols. Does the faculty body, as a whole, believe in the ability of all students to learn, or do they view themselves as dispensers of information in which students either understand content or do not? We looked at the empirical evidence suggesting a direct correlation between a building's collective efficacy and student achievement, faculty happiness, and attrition. Finally, we examined ways administrators can measure collective efficacy and ways in which they can engage faculty to change it.

A common thread running through this chapter on teacher efficacy has been the critical role principals and administrators play in influencing not only a specific teacher's level of self-efficacy but the collective efficacy of their building. The climate which a principal influences often determines whether teachers feel empowered in important policy decisions, their concerns and needs are heard, they are given adequate resources (e.g., materials and professional development) to do their job well, and that the primary goal of the building is student achievement. If collective efficacy drops, or student achievement falls, remedies can only occur with administrative support and direction. Working together, administrators and teachers can not only dream the big ideas, they can work together to insure their goals are achieved.

DISCUSSION QUESTIONS

1. Complete a teacher self-efficacy instrument. Are you surprised by the results? What do the results tell you about your strengths and weaknesses? What can you do to strengthen your efficacy score?

2. Based on your experiences and observation, how would you gauge the collective efficacy of your building?

3. What would you like to see done by your principal or school leaders to enhance collective efficacy in your building?

4. How do you think teacher self-efficacy affects a teacher's instruction?

5. Do you think your (and other teachers') self-efficacy affects student achievement? How?

6. What examples can you provide in which your level of self-efficacy in a particular area affected your students' achievement?

NOTE

1. The interested reader is referred to Tschannen-Moran and Hoy (2001) for a detailed discussion of the history of the development of teacher self-efficacy scales from the Rand Studies in the late 1970s until the early 2000s.

REFERENCES

Allinder, R. M. (1995). An examination of the relationship between teacher efficacy and curriculum-based measurement and student achievement. *Remedial and Special Education, 16*, 247–254.

Armor, D., Conry-Oseguera, P., Cox, M., King, N., McDonnell, L., Pascal, A., … Zellman, G. (1976). *Analysis of the school preferred reading program in selected Los Angeles minority schools* (Report No. R-2007-LAUSD). Santa Monica, CA: The Rand Corporation, Los Angeles, CA. (ERIC Document Reproduction Services No. 130 243)

Ashton, P. (1985). Motivation and the teacher's sense of efficacy. In C. Ames & R. Ames (Eds.), *Research on motivation in education* (Vol. 2, pp. 141–171). Orlando, FL: Academic Press.

Ashton, P. T., Olejnik, S., Crocker, L., & McAuliffe, M. (1982). *Measurement problems in the study of teachers' sense of efficacy.* Paper presented at the annual meeting of the American Educational Research Association, New York, NY.

Avanzi, L., Miglioette, M., Velasco, V., & Balduci, C. (2013). Cross-validation of the Norwegian Teacher's Self-Efficacy Scale. *Teaching & Teacher Education, 31*(1), 69–78.

Bandura, A. (1977). Self-efficacy: Toward a unifying theory of behavior change. *Psychological Review, 84*(2), 191–215.

Bandura, A. (1986). *Social foundations of thought and action: A social cognitive theory.* Englewood Cliffs, NJ: Prentice-Hall.

Bandura, A. (1993). Perceived self-efficacy in cognitive development and functioning. *Educational Psychologist, 28*(2), 117–148.

Bandura, A. (1997). *Self-efficacy: The exercise of control.* New York, NY: W. H. Freeman.

Barouch Gilbert, R., Adesope, O. O., & Schroeder, N. L. (2013). Efficacy beliefs, job satisfaction, stress and their influence on the occupational commitment of English-medium content teachers in the Dominican Republic. *Educational Psychology, 34*(7), 876–899.

Berman, P., McLaughlin, M. W., Bass, G., Pauly, E., & Zellman, G. (1977). *Federal programs supporting educational change: Vol. 7. Factors affecting implementation and continuation.* Los Angeles, CA: The Rand Corporation. (ERIC Document Reproduction Service No. 140 432)

Brinson, D., & Steiner, L. (2007). *Building collective efficacy: How leaders inspire teachers to achieve* (Issue Brief). Washington, DC: Center for Comprehensive School Reform and Improvement.

Bouffard-Bouchard, T., Parent, S., & Larivee, S. (1991). Influence of self-efficacy on self-regulation and performance among junior and senior high school age students. *International Journal of Behavior Development, 14,* 153–164.

Canrinus, E. T., Helms-Lorenz, M., Beijaart, D., Buitnik, J., & Hofman, A. (2012). Self-efficacy, job satisfaction, motivation, and commitment: Exploring the relationships between indicators of teachers' professional identity. *European Journal of Psychology in Education, 27*(1), 115–132.

Caprara, G., Barbaranelli, C., Steca, P., & Malone, P. (2006). Teachers' self-efficacy beliefs as determinants of job satisfaction and students' academic achievement: A study at the school level. *Journal of School Psychology, 44,* 473–490.

Collie, R. J., Shapka, J. D., & Perrey, N. E. (2012). School climate and social-emotional learning: Predicting teacher stress, job satisfaction, and teaching efficacy. *Journal of Educational Psychology, 104,* 1189–1204.

Chang, I.-H. (2011). A study of the relationships between distributed leadership, teacher academic optimism and student achievement in Taiwanese elementary schools. *School Leadership & Management, 31*(5), 491–515.

Chong, W., Klassen, R. M., Huan, V., Wong, I., & Kates, A. D. (2010). The relationships among school types, teacher efficacy beliefs, and academic climate: Perspective from Asian middle schools. *The Journal of Educational Research, 103,* 183–190.

Gibson, S., & Dembo, M. (1984). Teacher efficacy: A construct validation. *Journal of Educational Psychology, 76,* 569–582.

Goddard, R. D., Hoy, W. K., & Hoy, A. W. (2000). Collective teacher efficacy: Its meaning, measure, and impact on student achievement. *American Educational Research Journal, 37*(2), 479–507.

Gusky, T. R. (1981). Measurement of responsibility teachers assume for academic success and failures in the classroom. *Journal of Teacher Education, 32,* 44–51

Hamre, B. K. & Pianta, R. L. (2010). Classroom environments and developmental processes. In J. L. Meece & J. S. Eccle (Eds.), *Handbook of research on schools, schooling, and human development* (pp. 25–41) New York, NY: Routledge.

Hardré, P.L., Crowson, H. M., Debacker, T. K., & White, D. (2010). Predicting the academic motivation of rural high school students. *The Journal of Experimental Education, 75*(4), 247–269.

Henson, R. K. (2002). From adolescent angst to adulthood: Substantive implications and measurement dilemmas in the development of teacher efficacy research. *Educational Psychologist, 37,* 137–150.

Hickman, C. J. (1993). *The structure of instructional criteria in corporate settings.* Unpublished doctoral dissertation. University of Missouri-St. Louis.

Hines, M. T. (2008). The interactive effects of race and teacher self-efficacy on the achievement gap in school. *National Forum of Multicultural Issues Journal, 7*, 1–11.

Hoy, W. K., & Woolfolk, A. E. (1993). Teachers' sense of efficacy and the organizational health of schools. *Elementary School Journal, 93*, 356–372.

Hoy, A. W. & Spero, R. B. (2005). Changes in teacher efficacy during the early years of teaching: A comparison of four measures. *Teacher and Teacher Education, 21*, 343–356.

Huber, M. J., Fruth, J. D., Avila-John, A., & Lopez-Ramirez, E. (2016). Teacher self-efficacy and student outcomes: A transactional approach in prevention. *Journal of Education and Human Development, 5*(1), 46–54.

Klassen, R. M., & Chiu, M. M. (2011). The occupational commitment and intention to quit of practicing and pre-service teachers: Influence of self-efficacy, job stress, and teaching context. *Contemporary Educational Psychology, 36*, 114–129.

Jimmieson, N. L., Hannam, R. L., & Yeo, G. B. (2010), Teacher organizational citizenship behaviours and job efficacy: Implications for student quality of school life. *British Journal of Psychology, 101*, 453–479.

Labone, E. (2004). Teacher efficacy: Maturing the construct through research in alternative paradigms. *Teaching and Teacher Education, 20*, 341–359.

Maslach, C., & Jackson, S. E. (1981). The measurement of experienced burnout. *Journal of Occupational Behavior, 2*, 99–113.

Midgley, C., Feldlaufer, H., & Eccles, J. S. (1989). Change in teacher efficacy and student self- and task-related beliefs in mathematics during the transition to junior high school. *Journal of Educational Psychology, 81*(2), 247–258.

Mohamadi, S. F., & Asadzadeh, H. (2011). Testing the mediating role of teachers' self-efficacy beliefs in the relationship between sources of efficacy information and students achievement. *Asia Pacific Education Review, 13*, 437–433.

Mojavezi, A., & Poodineh Tamiz, M. (2012). The impact of teacher self-efficacy on the students' motivation and achievement. *Theory and Practices in Language Studies, 2*(3), 483–491.

Moore, W., & Esselman, M. (1992). *Teacher efficacy, power, school climate and achievement: A desegregating district's experience.* Paper presented at the annual meeting of the American Educational Research Association, San Francisco, CA.

O'Neill, S. C., & Stephenson, J. (2011). The measurement of classroom management self-efficacy: A review of measurement instrument development and influences. *Educational Psychology, 31*, 261–299.

Protheroe, N. (2008, May–June). Teacher efficacy: What is it and does it matter? *Principal,* 42–45.

Rose, J. S., & Medway, F. J. (1981). Measurement of teachers' beliefs in their control over student outcome. *Journal of Educational Research, 74*, 185–190.

Ross, J. A. (1992). Teacher efficacy and the effect of coaching on student achievement. *Canadian Journal of Education, 17*(1), 51–65.

Ross, J. A. (1994, June). *Beliefs that make a difference: The origins and impacts of teacher efficacy.* Paper presented at the annual meeting of the Canadian Association for Curriculum Studies, Calgary, Alberta, Canada.

Ross, J. & Bruce, C. (2007a). Professional development effects on teacher efficacy: Results of randomized field trial. *The Journal of Educational Research, 101*(1), 50–60.

Ross, J. A., & Bruce, C. D. (2007b). Teacher self-assessment: A mechanism for facilitating professional growth. *Teaching and Teacher Education, 23*, 146–159.

Ross, J. A., & Gray, P. (2006). Transformational leadership and teacher commitment to organizational values: The mediating effects of collective teacher efficacy. *School Effectiveness and School Improvement, 17*(2), 179–199.

Rotter, J. B. (1966). Generalized expectances for internal versus external control of reinforcement. *Psychological Monographs, 80*(1), 1–28.

Salanova, M., Llorns, S., & Schaufeli, W. B. (2012). "Yes, I can, I fell good, and I just do it!" On gain cycles and spirals of efficacy beliefs, affect, and Engagement. *Applied Psychology: An International Review, 60*(2), 255–285.

Savas, A. C., Bozgeyik, Y., & Eser, I. (2014). A study on the relationship between teacher self-efficacy and burnout. *European Journal of Educational Research, 3*(4), 159–166.

Schwarzer, R., & Hallum, S. (2008). Perceived teacher self-efficacy as a predictor of job stress and burnout: Mediation analysis. *Applied Psychology: An International Review, 57*, 152–171.

Siegle, D., & McCoach, D. B. (2007). Increasing student mathematics through teacher training. *Journal of Advanced Academics, 18*(2), 278–312.

Sherman, H., Hickman, C., & Basile, C. (2015). Transforming educator preparation programs and perspectives. *World Universities Forum, 8*(2), 22–28.

Throndsen, I., & Turmo, A. (2013). Primary mathematics teachers' goal orientations and student achievement. *Instructional Science: An International Journal of the Learning Sciences, 41*(2), 307–322.

Tschannen-Moran, A., & Hoy, A. W. (2001). Teacher efficacy: Capturing an elusive construct. *Teacher and Teacher Education, 17*, 783–805. Retrieved from https://doi.org/10.1016/S0742-051X(01)00036-1

Tschannen-Moran, A., Hoy, W., & Hoy, W. K. (1998). Teacher efficacy: Its meaning and measure. *Review of Educational Research, 68*(2), 202–248.

Thoonen, E. E. J., Sleegers, P. J. C., Peetsma, T. T. D., & Oort, F. J. (2011). Can teachers motivate students to learn? *Educational Studies, 37*, 345–360.

Ware, H., & Kitsantas, A. (2007). Teacher and collective efficacy beliefs as predictors of professional commitment. *The Journal of Educational Research, 100*(5), 303–310.

Watson, S. (1991). *A study of the effects of teacher efficacy on the academic achievement of third-grade students in selected elementary schools in South Carolina.* Unpublished doctoral dissertation, South Carolina State College, Orangebury.

Woolfolk Hoy, A., Hoy, W. K., & Kurz, N. (2008). Teacher's academic optimism: The development and test of a new construct. *Teaching and Teacher Education, 24*, 821–834.

Woolfolk-Hoy, A., Rasoff, B., & Hoy, W. K. (1990). Prospective teachers' sense of efficacy and beliefs about control. *Journal of Educational Psychology, 82*(1), 81–91.

Zee, M., & Koomen, H. M. Y. (2016). Teacher self-efficacy and its effects on classroom processes, student academic adjustment, and teacher well-being: A synthesis of 40 years of research. *Review of Educational Research, 86*(4), 981–1015.

CHAPTER 5

PARENTS' ROLE IN FOSTERING MATHEMATICAL SELF-EFFICACY

Parents and Teachers Working Together

Education is often viewed as a triad among teachers, students, and students' parents.[1] Thus far, we have examined the role self-efficacy plays in the motivation of students to persevere in increasingly complex subjects. We have also examined the role self-efficacy plays in teacher effectiveness and its critically important impact on teachers' beliefs regarding their competence to affect mathematics learning. The third part of the triad—parents—also requires attention. If nurtured properly, parents can be a powerful ally in fostering students' self-efficacy at home as well as school. This alliance between teacher and parents may not come naturally, though, and may require thoughtful dedication on the part of the teacher (including the administration) to intentionally increase parental involvement. Procedural questions, such as how much involvement teachers want the parents to have, including when, how often, and in what form, need to be addressed, usually in concert with other teachers and building/district administrators.

This chapter begins by examining what we know about the traditional role of parents in their child's education, and how various assumptions some teachers make may not be supported by evidence. We then look at parental self-efficacy and how that can affect teacher engagement and

Learning Mathematics Successfully: Raising Self-Efficacy in Students, Teachers, and Parents
pp. 107–123
Copyright © 2019 by Information Age Publishing

student learning. Finally, we examine concrete ways teachers can constructively engage parents in reinforcing learning objectives. As well, we discuss strategies teachers can use to heighten not only the parent's level of efficacy, but those appropriate for increasing their child's self-efficacy.

PREDICTORS OF PARENTAL INVOLVEMENT

Many teachers, and district administrators, strive to involve parents in the child's education. The frequency and nature of that participation, though, often varies among teachers and districts. Some teachers may adopt an "I'll take what I can get of parents' time" approach; some may work hard to create varied opportunities to engage parents; and others may shun parental involvement because of prior unproductive experiences, time on task concerns or cautious about parents who may be too assertive (Andersen & Minke, 2007; Bandura, Barbaranelli, Caprana, and Pastorelli, 2001; Hoover-Dempsey, Bassler, & Brissie, 1987; Peiffer, 2015; Pajeres, 2005). The variety of interactions and results affect the extent to which parents and teachers feel comfortable engaging with each other.

Hoover-Dempsey and Sandler (1997) identified three main predictors of parental involvement: *parental role construction*, *parental self-efficacy*, and *general invitations*. Parental role construction pertains to roles parents adopt to guide them in being involved in their child's education. These roles are frequently adopted through group expectations and cultural norms of parents' environments, for example, other parents at the child's school, parents' workplace, the community, and the family. Often these groups influence parents' concepts of their role and involvement in their child's education. If the demands and expectations are high, parents will tend to become more engaged in educational activities and progress. Conversely, if the groups with which parents belong expect little or no parental involvement, parents are less likely to become involved in educational activities.

It is important for teachers to be aware of the general role construction of parents. Teachers may find that some parents are conflicted by wanting more involvement, but have time constraints or job demands. Others may have different cultural philosophies regarding parental involvement and roles, such as questioning who has the responsibility and authority for disciplining a child, teaching the child social manners, and whose responsibility it is to initiate parental involvement with the school (Hoover-Dempsey & Sandler, 1997). Teachers can more easily understand parents' child-rearing philosophies and strategize appropriate ways to engage with their child's educational activities when understanding parents' general role construction.

It is important to note that role construction varies by students' ages. Younger students' parents tend to be more actively involved in their child's education. However, the connection tends to wane as children advance to higher grades. This change can be related to increasingly difficult academic content, varied student/teacher relationships in middle and high school, and/or the increased desire for students to be more independent. Usually, less frequent parental involvement after middle school tends to follow common developmental patterns.

Parental self-efficacy pertains to parents' beliefs that they can exert positive influences on their child's educational progress. These beliefs are rooted in three factors (Eccles & Harold, 1993): First is the parent's beliefs about whether they can help their student with school work, second, the parents' views of their competence as students progress through higher grade levels and, third, the parents' beliefs that they can influence school policy and governance. Self-efficacy theory suggests that parents will make involvement decisions by thinking through the likely outcomes of their actions. The stronger the self-efficacy, the higher the goals become, and the firmer the parent becomes in meeting them (Bandura, 1989; Hoover-Dempsey & Sandler, 1997). That is, the process of setting goals (such as attending parent-teacher conferences, understanding their child's content and how it is taught, establishing regular contact with teachers to discuss progress, or requests for personalized attention) is influenced by parents' appraisals and estimates of their capabilities in this situation. Parental self-efficacy also influences tenacity in following through with goals in the face of failure and obstacles. Self-efficacy is not necessarily concerned with "skills" but a belief that one can employ whatever subskills one possesses to achieve the goal (Bandura, 1989). Thus, it is not surprising that parents with less resources and lower educational levels can and do act efficaciously to involve themselves in their children's educational activities when they believe in their ability to influence their child's progress (Bandura, 1997; Clark, 1983; Scott-Jones, 1897; Segal, 1985).

Conversely, parents with low levels of self-efficacy tend to set lower goals for themselves and their student, have fewer interactions with the school, and do not generally believe that they can influence either the teacher, school, or their child's progress (Bandura, 1997; Hoover-Dempsey & Sandler, 1997). Such beliefs can stem from feelings of incompetence regarding their child's curriculum; an inability to identify or articulate problems their child might be having; a belief that it is "up to the teacher" to teach; or simply knowing that there is no time to be adequately involved. These thought patterns may lead parents to shun interactions with school related activities, or to quickly give up trying when met with any obstacle, resistance or failure. Sometimes these feelings are rooted in previous negative experiences of their own with teachers and schools, and sometimes they are rooted in lack of time or desire to "interfere" with "the teacher's work."

Teachers cannot assume the self-efficacy level of their students' parents based on socioeconomic status nor level of parent education (Bandura, 1997). Parents will fall widely on the self-efficacy continuum regardless of these variables. Teachers can, however, informally assess a parent's level of self-efficacy and work to heighten it, if needed. Strategies for doing this will be discussed later in this chapter.

Table 5.1 identifies common characteristics of parents possessing high and low levels of parental self-efficacy. These are general traits, and not meant to be exhaustive. Moreover, since self-efficacy pertains to specific beliefs about specific behaviors, it is possible to be highly efficacious in one or more trait, and weak in others, although that situation is less common. Nevertheless, it is incumbent on teachers not to make universal assumptions about parents based on a few traits. Teachers get a truer sense of parents' strengths and weaknesses and their willingness to align with educators' goals of parental involvement by exploring parents' philosophies of, and roles in, their child's education. Indeed, these "teacher goals" of involvement are frequently driven by their own sense of self-efficacy, the implications of which are discussed in the next section.

The third predictor of parental involvement, general invitations, pertains to the fundamental question: Do parents perceive that the child and school want them involved (Hoover-Dempsey & Sandler, 1997)? Epstein and Dauber (1991) found that teachers who actively and persistently invited parents to participate in their child's schooling yielded greater participation than those who did not. Highly involved parents also tended to have more positive feelings both about the school and the teacher (Epstein, 1986), had students with higher reading achievement (Epstein, 1991), and fostered beliefs in parents of the overall "goodness" of the school (Daube & Epstein, 1993). Moreover, Eccles and Harold (1994) found that these positive influences spanned across all socioeconomic conditions.

Anderson and Minke (2007) also found that specific invitations from teachers to participate in a child's schooling was particularly important among minority parents. As well, resource barriers such as time, transportation, and childcare did not affect whether or not African American parents chose to become engaged with the school. Their findings also suggested that minority parents' involvement with their child's schooling tended to be more focused on the home, as opposed to coming to the school building. The researchers caution teachers and administrators not to gauge parental involvement solely on what is visible to them (e.g. attending parent-teacher conferences or volunteering), but to inquire

**Table 5.1. Common Traits Exhibited by Parents
Possessing High Versus Low Levels of Parental Self-Efficacy**

Variable	High Parental Self-Efficacy	Low Parental Self-Efficacy
Setting goals for their participation in child's education and for the child's success	Thought out and realistic goals that involve teacher-parent contact. Proactively plans activities that lead to success.	No planned goals, but may react to teacher or school if contacted. Defaults to teacher and school to determine curriculum and activities that lead to learning.
Involvement in child's activities	Highly involved. Regular contact with the teacher offering curricular activities, solicited or not. Involved with child's school work and believes they are a partner with the teacher to insure the child's success in learning the content.	Awareness of child's school work and the curriculum may be vague to non-existent. Tends to shun contact with the teacher or school, preferring to "leave education to the teacher." Does not believe they have the time nor expertise to be a "second teacher" to their child.
Involvement with school/teachers	Regular, and frequently parent-initiated.	Rare, and only when contacted by the teacher or school.
Viewing intelligence	Believes intelligence is malleable and is a function of persistence and effort. They believe their child can learn even the most difficult subjects with quality instruction and proper effort and persistence.	Views intelligence as fixed, and a function of ability and luck. They believe their child has "abilities" in some subjects, and not in others and that inordinate "effort" and "persistence" will only frustrate the child.
Helping child "get along" in social situations and problem-solve	Actively encourages child to think-through solutions to a problem, and work around obstacles. Views problems as something to solve, and encourages identifying multiple possible solutions. Failures, conflicts and obstacles are viewed as something to solve, not "live with."	Tends to offer fewer solutions, and often encourages the child to accept "that's the way it is." Problems and conflicts are viewed pragmatically whereby they are solved, if possible, or accepted as reality. Parents default to a hands-off approach and let the school, teacher, or student solve difficulties.

with parents about nonvisible form of engagement in the home, such as conversations with students about their work, parental assistance with school work, arrangement of private tutoring, and other forms of informal engagement.

Many factors, as well as school invitations are key for involving families. Other considerations are students' ages and parents' perception of their child's academic progress. Daube and Epstein (1993) and Delgado-Gaitan (1992) found a positive correlation between high-achieving students and parental involvement among elementary students, with less involvement among struggling students. Baker and Stevenson (1986), however, found the opposite correlations among adolescent middle-school students, Parents of struggling students were more involved with their education than higher achieving students. One possible explanation is that, as children matriculated through the school system, parents were more apt to become involved only when they discovered students were struggling with content. Parents became less inclined to take an active role in their schooling for students performing on or above grade level (Hoover-Dempsey & Sandler, 1997). In general, however, most seasoned teachers will attest— and research findings confirm—that parental enthusiasm for active involvement in their child's schooling declines as the child progresses through the school system (Hoover-Dempsey & Sandler, 1997).

Teacher Self-Efficacy and Invitations for Parent Involvement.   Chapter 4 discussed the varied aspects of teacher self-efficacy, including implications for a teacher's desire to involve parents. We examined how teachers possessing high levels of self-efficacy tend to welcome parent involvement, and intentionally devise ways to communicate, answer questions, and forge a partnership with parents toward to the common goal of student learning. Conversely, teachers with low self-efficacy tend to shun parental involvement, perhaps fearing a challenge to their competence, or being unsure what the proper boundaries are between the parent and teacher (Bandura, 1997; Ross & Gray, 2006).

Hoover-Dempsey et al. (1987) studied the effects of teacher self-efficacy on parental involvement in 78 schools in eight districts. They found significant correlations between high teacher self-efficacy and parental involvement in conferences, parent volunteering, tutoring, and teacher perceptions of support. Whereas correlations cannot be viewed as causation, findings imply that high levels of teacher efficacy have a beneficial effect on these engagement variables. Hoover-Dempsey et al. (1987) theorize that high teacher self-efficacy manifests as a level of professionalism and confidence making it more possible that teachers can discuss their program and goals with families. Moreover, parents can feel their time was well spent when encouraged to ask questions and convey useful information about their child. Additionally, efficacious teachers are able to convey requests for parental help as compliments to the coursework rather than teacher inadequacy. Lastly, teachers with high levels of self-efficacy can also work to increase teachers' and parents' sense of role differentiation, thus minimizing potential threats to roles or expertise that sometimes happens with parent-teacher interactions.

Collective efficacy is also a broad concern regarding parental involvement (Ross & Gray, 2006). Teachers' efforts to involve families are highly effective. As well, teachers can contribute to a positive school climate to enhance individual communication initiatives and schools and districts can work together to establish norms of practice for positive, consistent and research based interactions. Principals and district administrators can guide professional development focused on student learning, with input from parents and teachers. The following questions suggest relevant and important topics for schools' and districts' consideration:

- What are the practices and philosophies in place now?
- What are teachers' levels of self-efficacy regarding communicating with and involving parents?
- What are the goals of involving parents? For example, one obvious goal is to forge a partnership with parents to reinforce the content of the courses. Other goals could be having a relationship built to ease any future problematic communication, creating goodwill toward the school/district, and helping parents understand how they can be helpful, thereby enabling them to be better parents.
- How do parents place on the Role Construction and Parental Self-Efficacy scale? How can we find out? What opportunities can we provide that persuades a more affirmative role construction for involvement and/or heightened parental self-efficacy?
- How can involving parents be constructive? What are the boundaries? How do we prevent this from being inordinately time consuming?
- What are different ways we can involve parents? Examples could include, parent-teacher conferences, one-on-one conversations about their child's progress, surveys asking about their and their child's satisfaction with school, and email or postal-mail blasts to all parents.
- How can we involve parents who have logistical issues like time or transportation constraints? How do we address parents who shun involvement with the school?
- What, if any, are the risks of persistently reaching out to parents requesting their involvement?
- How is success measured in terms of parental involvement and student achievement?

Relative Strength of the Three Predictors.   This section discussed role construction, parental self-efficacy, and general invitations as three primary predictors of parental involvement. Of the three, role construction is generally perceived to be the most powerful of the three predictors as it answers the critical question, "*Should* I be involved?" Parental self-efficacy, "*Can* I be involved?" is a powerful adjunct to role construction because it encourages involvement *if* the parent feels that is their role (Hoover-Dempsey & Sandler, 1997). Parents' enthusiasm for involvement will diminish if they feel they should not or cannot be involved. If both of these predictors are in place, chances dramatically increase that parents will welcome becoming involved with their child's education.

General Invitations, while important, is the weakest of the three predictors (Hoover-Dempsey & Sandler, 1997). Invitations and other deliberate ways to involve parents (e.g., conferences, meetings, briefings, home visits) are specific mechanisms by which interested parents engage with the teacher. In the absence of affirmative role construction and parental self-efficacy, though, these invitations may not be readily accepted. However, parents who answer "Yes" to "Should I be involved?" and have high parental self-efficacy will tend to involve themselves in their child's education, with or without an invitation or formal engagement mechanism from the teacher.

ENHANCING PARENTAL SELF-EFFICACY

Scholarly research into the parents' role in fostering the self-efficacy of young people has mushroomed in the last 2 decades. In 2018, for example, a simple Internet search for "parental self-efficacy" yielded 2.4 million hits. Teachers can frequently be aware of their own and their students' levels of self-efficacy. Of interest is also how parents' levels of self-efficacy affect their child. What can a faculty (or individual teachers) do to enhance parental self-efficacy?

Parental self-efficacy not only influences whether (and how much) a parent engages with the school, but also influences the types and quality of parent-child interactions such as setting goals, persistence, and coping strategies. Indeed, parents may be children's most important role model. Parents influence their children through modeling, engaging in their own learning, reading, asking about the school day, what they are learning, and messages regarding success or failure (Hoover-Demsey et al., 1997; Pfeiffer, 2015) Bandura et al. (2001) found that children's and parents' academic efficacy are correlated with their own scholastic aspirations, achievement and social efficacy.

Teacher's sensitivity to the critical role parental self-efficacy plays is an important role in understanding students' educational environments. Opportunities can be created that help parents not only improve their own levels of self-efficacy, but help parents engage in behaviors and feedback that heighten their child's as well. The goal is to foster an alliance with parents to reinforce the teacher's self-efficacy strategies with consistent and effective messages outside of the school day.

The literature contains several published self-efficacy scales for parents (e.g., Hoover-Dempsey, 2005) that teachers can give to parents, or parents can take alone for their own information. Appendix B of this book contains our own informal parent self-efficacy scale to assist faculty or parents in having conversations about the parent's confidence in assisting their child either academically, or navigating school life. Scored on a 6-point Likert scale from *strongly disagree* to *strongly agree*, this scale informs teachers as to the self-efficacy levels of their students' parents. The form can be used in large parent-involvement programs, or can be used one on one in parent-teacher conferences. Since the form consists of ten straightforward questions, a teacher could also use the instrument by asking several of the items in informal conversation. The 10 items are:

- I believe that I can help my child with their schoolwork.
- I believe that I can instill in my child the value of education.
- I believe that I can guide my child to avoid disciplinary problems.
- When my child experiences academic difficulties, I know how to guide them through it.
- If I need to, I know how to effectively deal with the teacher and/or school to solve problems.
- I know when to step in, and when to back off in helping my child with schoolwork.
- I know how to draw the connection between success in school and success in life for my child.
- If I am confused or do not know how to handle a parenting issue, I know who to contact for help.
- I am familiar with my child's lessons and know how to help if needed.
- I can prevent my child from falling under the influence of the wrong crowd.

The answers to these questions can guide teachers in productive conversations with parents about ways to reinforce teachers' efforts and strategies to instill confidence in students. Such techniques include attributing a grade for effort and persistence, as opposed to ability or luck, setting realistic goals and providing coping strategies for students when frustrated with an assignment.

Faculty can design research-based parent involvement programs on the development of self-efficacy to better ensure that it is based on growth from measured academic progress (Pfeiffer, 2015). If schools help parents increase their self-efficacy, parents may improve their own coping behaviors and be able to stick with tasks longer, such as spending more time with their children on schoolwork (Bandura & Locke, 2003). Such parent-involvement programs would follow the tenets of efficacy acquisition, such as observing the modeling of productive parent-child conversations, feedback, and setting goals. Self-efficacy can be taught, through observation and modeling, and these types of parental involvement programs can enhance a parents' role construction (What should I be doing?) as well as their level of self-efficacy (What can I do?).

IMPLICATIONS FOR TEACHERS AND PARENTS

The goal of parental-education programs should be to inform parents of the teachers' strategies to increase their students' levels of self-efficacy and to make parents a partner in reinforcing these efforts. This can only be done with clear communication between the teacher(s) and parents, as well as agreement on the appropriateness of the strategy. Frank Pajares (2005) offers over 30 suggestions in which parents and teachers can strategize together to reinforce a young person's self-efficacy. The recommendations fit broadly into categories of parental behaviors, adjusting children's attitudes, goal setting, and how to think about success and failure. These strategies can guide teachers into productive conversations with parents about how parents interact with their child. They can also serve as a reminder to teachers about their own interaction with their students throughout the day.

Parental Behaviors. "Parental behaviors" is a broad category and actually affects most of the strategies contained in this section. In this context, however, we emphasize specific parental behaviors that are instrumental in fostering self-efficacy in their student. Table 5.2 identifies recommendations and action steps for parents enhancing self-efficacy in their student.

Adjusting Children's Attitudes. Efficacious teachers and parents identify problematic attitudes that some children develop and actively work toward guiding those attitudes toward a heightened self-efficacy perspective. Table 5.3 provides examples of common attitudes for which parents can play critical roles in modifying.

Goal Setting. Often, the difference between highly efficacious teachers and parents and low efficacious ones is the extent to which they set realistic and obtainable goals for themselves and help their child set their own

**Table 5.2.   Action Steps for Parents
to Enhance Self-Efficacy in Their Student**

Recommendation	*Action*
Model the behavior you are seeking	• Be an active learner who is inquisitive and persistent in learning new skills • Be open and public about problem-solving • Reinforce the message that "there is an answer to this"
Beware of helping too much	• Be an "instrumental" resource to help guide toward a solution, without giving them the answer and to encourage self-reliance • Avoid being an "executive" helper who provides an immediate solution to a problem or question
Be careful with language	• Use positive messages rather than commiserating with phrases such as "I'm not a math person, either" • Saying "Let's work on this together—we can figure this out" or "There's an answer to this problem, let's work through the steps to see where you're confused" send a message of confidence in the student that persistence is required
Inquire into student's self-efficacy	• Students can harbor and hide insecurities and lack of confidence • Simple questions such as "How are you feeling about adding fractions?" or "Tell me the most difficult thing you deal with throughout the day" can give a glimpse into a student's confidence level
Self-efficacy is contagious	• Cultivate student potential by making time for them, answering questions, creating an emotional closeness, and openly communicate • Monitor, support and guide students as needed to productive and constructive personal and academic goals

Source: Pajares (2005).

objectives. While goal setting is critical in directing energies toward important outcomes, setting the wrong types, or unrealistic, goals can be worse than not setting goals at all. Table 5.4 provides recommendations and actions for helping children set goals.

Thinking About Success and Failure.   Each of us experiences a fair share of success and failure throughout life. How we attribute success and rebound from failures often determines how adaptive we are to life's issues and how resilient we are in meeting the next challenge. Guiding students toward an efficacious position in dealing with success and failures teaches them lifelong skills toward being the most productive person possible. Table 5.5 provides examples of how parents and teachers can guide their students on how to think about success and failure, and the importance of this being a lifelong process.

Table 5.3.   Aligning Student Attitudes
Toward an Efficacious Perspective

Attitude	*Action*
Skill development versus self-enhancement	• Skill development refers to a student's mastery of content; self-enhancement refers to their self-esteem and how good they feel about themselves. Goal of education should be skill development, accomplished through mastery of content. • Self-efficacy is developed by successfully mastering a skill with academic challenges. • Good feelings stem from successfully mastering academic work, not by doing mediocre work on an easy task. • Know how much challenge students can undertake without becoming frustrated or burned out.
Praise only that which is praiseworthy	• Praising a student for a job well done, especially one that is perceived as challenging is an important way to show encouragement or support. • Feedback and persuasion influence the formation of self-efficacy concepts, so parents should be conscious of providing praise and reward. • Directly connect praise and reward to behaviors that justify this feedback.
Praise effort, not ability	• Praise effort and persistence because they are key ingredients to successfully mastering challenging subjects and ability to perform. • If only ability is praised, a student can miss the connection between effort and mastery, and assume that frustrations and failures are attributable to lack of ability, instead of lack of effort.
Challenge under-confidence—everyone, on occasion, doubts their abilities.	• Recognize common and reasonable doubts with new material, from self-defeating doubts that are not reasonable or are exaggerated. • Continually challenge doubts that students exhibit, whenever they form. • Provide exercises students can master to gain confidence. Continue to praise effort that leads to success.

Source: Pajares (2005).

In his chapter "Self-Efficacy During Childhood and Adolescence," Frank Pajares (2005) offers some caveats for these and other educational suggestions and precepts offered for consideration. First, any suggestion, or precept, should not be viewed as a principle or rule to be adopted independent of context. These ideas are merely a "starting point" by which parents and teachers may seek solutions to the challenges they face. These ideas, though, must be tested against the reality of a particular school and the students comprising that school.

A second word of caution revolves around a too-often perception that an emphasis on self-esteem, confidence, self-efficacy and personal

Table 5.4. Parents Helping Children Set Goals

Recommendation	*Action*
• Set short-term versus long-term goals because long-term goals for children can be overwhelming and difficult on a student's motivation. Setting short-term goals are more digestible, allowing larger tasks to be broken down into manageable pieces.	• Create ways for students to learn, early on, to approach tasks by breaking them down to components and doing those. • Students generalize this skill to future tasks.
• Provide help in getting goals. Setting goals is a learned skill, not an innate ability.	• Students, especially in elementary and middle school, need help and guidance in setting goals. • Goals should be realistic, obtainable, challenging, and specific, within a set time frame. • Teachers help parents set realistic goals such as, "I will talk to my child about their math homework every night and check their work for accuracy."
• Set mastery goals, rather than performance goals. • Mastery goals emphasize learning to master concepts, overcome challenges, and learning as an end it itself. Performance goals emphasize being better than others, appearing smart, or avoiding looking incompetent. • Students with a master-goal orientation tend to persist longer with challenging work, have higher self-efficacy, set high achievement goals, and delve deeper into subjects to understand them.	• Teachers can be instrumental in creating classroom climates in which mastery orientations are encouraged and ego-orientations discouraged. • Emphasize *learning* over *performing* so that students approach the curriculum with less anxiety and are more resourceful in solving problems and moving on from failures that inevitably arise.

Source: Pajares (2006).

achievement results in self-obsessed and self-centered students. Some believe these learners are then incapable of empathy, nurturing others, forming and maintain lasting relationships, or delaying gratification. As Pajares writes,

> When what is communicated to young people from an early age is that nothing matters quite as much as how they feel or how confident they should be, one can rest assured that the world will sooner or later teach them a lesson in humility that may not be easily learned. An obsession with one's sense of self is responsible for an alarming increase in depression and other mental difficulties. (p. 365)

Table 5.5.   Guiding Students to Think About Success and Failure

Recommendation	*Action*
Emphasize that success and failure is a product of effort and persistence, not ability or luck. Neither luck nor ability can be controlled by the student, but persistence and effort can.	• Use phrases such as "All that work you did on the fractions unit really paid off. Good job on working so hard!" sends the message that the *effort* is what is praiseworthy and attributes success to effort, and not ability (or luck). • Avoid messages that imply failure is due to lack of ability or bad luck.
Help students understand that your goals and expectations for them are reasonable and, with effort, they can succeed.	• Assure students that what might seem daunting and complicated is actually broken down into manageable chunks. • Avoid letting fear and doubts become a self-fulfilling prophecy. • Instill in students the belief that they can succeed (with persistence and effort).
Guide students toward a disciplined structure	• Design systems of studying, note taking, participating in class, and organizing and planning schoolwork to make these self-regulatory processes automatic and habitual as early as possible.
Generalize success. Students find that success in one area can more easily lead to success in other areas by connecting and discussing content areas.	• Create opportunities for students to make the connections between success in one area (e.g., measuring the math and science) and success in other areas (e.g., vocabulary in math and reading). • Continually emphasize the connection between strategies that solved previous math problems with strategies that will work with current problems.

Source: Pajares (2006).

However, transformations of schools, teaching practices, curriculum and parenting with a focus on the self-beliefs of students need not necessarily be incompatible with concern for their personal, social and psychological well-being and that "warranted self-confidence need not result in arrogant self-satisfaction" (Pajares, 2005, p. 366). Indeed, it is social, emotional and academic difficulties frequently brought on by misdirected motivation and lack of commitment that characterizes those labeled as underachievers, dropouts, "at risk," troublemaker, or delinquent as a consequence of beliefs they developed about their capabilities to exercise control over their environments.

Teachers and parents have a responsibility of preparing confident and fully functioning individuals capable of commanding their future and fulfilling their hopes and dreams. This can be done by nurturing a habit of excellence in the schoolwork and in their personal lives while at the same time nurturing beliefs that they possess the skills to address any obstacle to their goals. These traits carry well into adulthood and create productive citizens who hopefully pass along these skills to future generations as either parents or teachers themselves.

SUMMARY

This chapter explored the sometimes complex relationship between parent and teacher. We explored the common predictors of parental involvement in their child's education, namely, role construction, parental self-efficacy, and general invitations from the school to participate. We then delved more deeply into how high and low self-efficacious parents approach both parenting and their relationship with the school. We also looked at how to talk to parents about their self-efficacy and strategies teachers can take to work with parents to heighten it.

Lastly, we examined the implications of self-efficacy for both parents and teachers and what each can do to foster their students' self-efficacy at home and at school. These implications were focused on four broad areas: Parental behavior, adjusting children's attitudes, goal setting, and how to think about success and failure.

The focus of this chapter was to elucidate the important relationship between teacher and parent, a relationship that is sometimes tricky and sometimes frustrating on both sides. However, if the focus remains on the student, and the student's learning, it is the student who will gain the most by having a productive alliance, with shared goals and concerns, between the teacher and parent. This chapter offered concrete strategies to help both teachers and parents achieve these goals.

DISCUSSION QUESTIONS

1. How would you rate your interactions with parents now? Productive? Minimal? Lacking? Excellent?
2. What are concrete things you would change about your relationships with parents?
3. How important do you feel an alliance with parents is?
4. What are the most imposing obstacles you see in developing the optimal parent relationship?

5.   How would you go about assessing parents' level of self-efficacy? What strategies would you employ to raise it, if needed?

6.   Of the "Implications for Parents and Teachers," which resonate the strongest with you? Which are you willing to try? Which do you (or your parents) already do well?

NOTE

1.   Throughout this chapter, "parent" refers to the primary caregiver of a student, whether that be a mother, father, grandparent, or other type of guardian.

REFERENCES

Anderson, K. J., & Minke, K. M. (2007). Parent involvement in education: Toward an understanding of parents' decision making. *The Journal of Educational Research, 100*(5), 311–323.

Bandura, A., Barbaranelli, C., Caprara, G. V., & Pastorelli, C. (2001). Self-efficacy beliefs as shapers of children's aspirations and career trajectories. *Child Development, 72*(1), 187–206.

Bandura, A., & Locke, E. (2003). Negative self-efficacy and goal effects revisited. *Journal of Applied Psychology, 88*(1), 87–99.

Bandura, A. (1989). Regulation of cognitive processes through perceived self-efficacy. *Developmental Psychology, 25*, 729–735.

Bandura, A. (1997). *Self-efficacy: The exercise of control.* New York, NY: W. H. Freeman & Company.

Clark, R. (1983). *Family life and school achievement: Why poor Black children succeed or fail.* Chicago, IL: University of Chicago Press.

Daube, S. L., & Epstein, J. L. (1993). Parents' attitudes and practices of involvement in inner-city elementary and middle schools. In N. F. Chavkin (Ed.), *Families and schools in a pluralistic society* (pp. 53–71). Albany, NY: State University of New York Press.

Delgado-Gaitan, C. (1992). School matters in the Mexican-American home: Socializing children to education. *American Educational Research Journal, 29*, 495–513.

Eccles, J. S., & Harold, R. D. (1993). Parent-school involvement during the early adolescent years. *Teacher College Record, 94*, 568–587.

Eccles, J. S., & Harold, R. D. (1994, October–November). *Family involvement in children's and adolescents' schooling.* Paper presented at the Family-School Links Conference, Pennsylvania State University.

Epstein, J. L. (1986). Parents' reactions to teacher practices of parent involvement. *Elementary School Journal, 86*, 277–294.

Epstein, J. L. (1991). Effects on student achievement of teachers' practices of parent involvement. In S. B. Silvern (Ed.), *Advances in reading/language research:*

Vol. 5. Literacy through family, community, and school interaction (pp. 261–276). Greenwich, CT: JAI Press.

Epstein, J. L., & Dauber, S. L. (1991). School programs and teacher practices of parent involvement in inner-city elementary and middle schools. *Elementary School Journal, 91,* 291–305.

Hoover-Dempsey, K.V. (2005). *Final performance report for OERI Grant # R305T010673: The social context of parental involvement: A path to enhanced achievement.* Washington, DC: U.S. Department of Education.

Hoover-Dempsey, K. V., Bassler, O. C., & Brissie, J. (1987). Parent involvement: Contributions of teacher efficacy, school socioeconomic status, and other school characteristics. *American Educational Research Journal, 24*(3), 417–435.

Hoover-Dempsey, K. V., & Sandler, H. M. (1997). Why do parents become involved in their children's education? *Review of Educational Research, 67*(1), 3–42.

Pajares, F. (2005). Self-efficacy during adolescence and childhood: Implications for teachers and parents. In F. Pajares & T. Urban (Eds.), *Self-efficacy beliefs of adolescents* (pp. 339–367). Greenwich, CT: Information Age.

Peiffer, G. D. (2015). *The effect of self-efficacy on parental involvement at the secondary school level.* Unpublished doctoral dissertation, University of Pittsburgh.

Ross, J. A., & Gray, P. (2006). Transformational leadership and teacher commitment to organizational values: The mediating effects of collective teacher efficacy. *School Effectiveness and School Improvement, 17*(2), 179–199.

Scott-Jones, D. (1991). Black families and literacy. In S. B. Silvern (Ed.), *Advances in reading/language research: A research annual. Literacy through family, community and school interaction* (pp. 173–200). Greenwich, CT: JAI Press.

Segal, M. (1985). A study of maternal beliefs and values within the context of an intervention program. In I. E. Sigel (Ed.), *Parental belief systems: The psychological consequences for children* (pp. 271–286). Hillsdale, NJ: Erlbaum.

CHAPTER 6

RAISING SELF-EFFICACY WITH MATHEMATICS GAMES AND ACTIVITIES

Increasing levels of self-efficacy when teaching and learning was discussed in previous chapters. Understanding and strengthening those connections can be accomplished in large part when students gain self-efficacy as they master content, skillfully use procedures and number facts, solve problems, and reason and value mathematics (Mathematics Learning Study Committee, 2001). An important additional factor in infusing self-efficacy in mathematics is that appreciation and enjoyment have been identified by the National Council of Teachers of Mathematics as a national goal for learning mathematics (Rutherford, 2015). Findings by the researcher, Ernest Afari (Afari, Algridge, & Fraser, 2012), suggest a strong and positive association among the learning environment, student enjoying their mathematics lessons and their academic efficacy. The objective of enjoying learning and enhancing of students' level of self-efficacy is vital to academic success.

One of the most common educational strategies to motivate and interest students in learning is integrating mathematics games in instruction. Games are identified as experiences that set rules and structure for play, add the element of chance to ability, provide a clear ending point or winning goal and challenge (Hays, 2005). Board games, card games and those drawn on paper or file folders, as well as computer-based experiences provide active learning opportunities and reinforce topics learned

Learning Mathematics Successfully: Raising Self-Efficacy in Students, Teachers, and Parents
pp. 125–145

in the classroom. Play can be competitive for points or other rewards or can be cooperative, requiring group work to solve problems. Just as with paper-based games, computer interactions can be individual or group based. Both formats of gaming activities, paper/pencil or technology based, tend to show learning because of the active learning components that are present in each (MacKenty, 2006; Sherman, Richardson, & Yard, 2013; Schrand, 2008). A list of highly effective websites for on line gaming is included in Appendix C. This chapter includes a variety of games ranging from those designed for one player to several individuals.

It is important to recognize that there is no evidence to indicate that games are the preferred instructional method in all situations. Instructional games, as research reports, should be embedded in instructional programs that include debriefing and feedback so that the learners understand what happened in the game and how these events support the instructional objectives (Afari, 2012; Vandercruysse, Vandewaetere, & Clarebout, 2012). That is, the most helpful games, when used to enhance instruction, are those in which the structure and rules of the games are based on mathematical ideas and winning is directly related to understanding the mathematics on which the game is based. Games are not the only teaching tool. They are also a vehicle for blending content and processes with developing confidence and belief in one's ability to succeed. Effectively mastering mathematics content, being encouraged by verbal persuasion and learning from others through vicarious experiences, all of which are self-efficacy influences, are all factors that impact the use of gaming in mathematics instruction.

CHARACTERISTICS OF EFFECTIVE GAMES

Challenging, interesting, and appealing math games feature the following specific attributes.

- Game Objective: The goal should be consistent and relatable to overall instructional objectives; it should be part of a larger instructional program. The paths to winning should be uncertain in that the learner should have to exert effort to achieve the goal.
- Differentiation: The game should include multiple levels of difficulty or complexity, so that all students may engage in some manner.
- Competition: Competition can be again a face-to-face, or a computer-controlled opponent, or against a criterion score.

- Interest: The game should embody emotional appeal and be age appropriate for the learners (Vandercruysse et al., 2012).

THE IMPACT OF SELF-EFFICACY

The four primary influences of self-efficacy on mathematics learners were described in Chapter 1. They are enactive mastery, vicarious experiences, verbal persuasion, and physiological states. These factors can impact students' progress in becoming more self-efficacious as they learn and practice mathematics with games. Opolot-Okurut (2010) suggested that teachers wishing to improve students' self-efficacy to mathematics should consider emphasizing student involvement and task organization. With more positive attitudes toward mathematics, it is possible that more students may choose to pursue mathematics-oriented classes in high school and college and mathematics-related careers.

The process and influence of "effective mastery" is evident as students practice, repeat basic fact computation and use rules to win games. For example, in the game described in this chapter "Play the Place to Win", students use place value, estimation, addition skills and number order to reason and win; the game contributes to the effective mastery of those concepts and procedures. When students replay the game, they repeat the same concepts and practices several times, improving their ability and moving toward mastery, in terms of their performance. Students are motivated, in an enjoyable and competitive or cooperative game format, to improve and gain confidence in their mathematics abilities.

Another influence on self-efficacy, verbal persuasion, is enhanced through game play. As students respond to encouragement and positive feedback, they are more likely to retain procedures. Positive feedback from other players and/or the teacher is task directed in terms of winning strategies or solutions; games provide an enjoyable and meaningful extension of the classroom instruction. Games have been shown to be more effective if they are followed by a debriefing session that highlights the importance of the game experiences in terms of instructional objectives (Cruz-Cunha, 2012). Research reports that while playing games, the students encouraged by their teachers to share ideas and help one another suggested greater student interactions during the mathematics lesson. Such interaction in the mathematics classroom has been recognized as the foundation for deep understanding, leading to more effective teaching and learning in mathematics (Ross, John, & Bruce, 2007). Analyses of the information gathered through interviews with students and teachers were used, in Afari's (Afari et al., 2012) study, to help to explain the statistically significant pretest–posttest differences for teacher support, involvement, personal relevance, enjoyment of mathematics lessons and academic efficacy scales. Analyses of students' interviews indicated that they viewed their teachers as being more supportive, approachable and interested in their learning after the use of games. Students agreed that mathematics was relevant to their lives. The study suggested that the games impacted positively on students' attitudes toward the learning of mathematics and their perceptions of some important aspects of classroom environment.

Vicarious learning impacts students as they watch others' strategies and decisions to try to win games and/ or cooperate with partners. Observing other players work together as they strategize, reason and problem solve in an enjoyable context is a powerful influence on self-efficacy. Games provide opportunities for children to work in small groups to not only cooperate or compete in solving mathematics problems, but also to observe authentic teamwork and effective communication. According to Franklin, Peat, and Lewis (2003), when students work on a gaming activity, "games foster group cooperation and typically create a high level of student involvement that makes them useful tools for effective teaching" (p. 82). Children learn from each other as they talk, share, and reflect throughout game times. These positive associations suggest practical ways in which the learning environment might be changed to enhance student attitudes.

INSTRUCTIONAL BENEFITS OF MATHEMATICS GAMES

Researchers Ke and Grabowski (2007) conducted a case study where 125 fifth graders participated in a cooperative team-games tournament. Games consisted of "skill exercises played during weekly tournaments" (p. 251). Students compete individually against other students and their winnings are brought back to their teams. This cooperative technique has been widely investigated and "research indicates that [team-games tournament] enhances students' academic achievement and attitudes toward the subject matter" (p. 251). These cooperative learning gaming methods tend to be successful because they "provide both group rewards and individual accountability" (p. 256). Studies by the early education researcher, Robert J. Marzano, explains that of the 60 studies he has been involved in regarding the effects of games on student achievement, "on average, using academic games in the classroom is associated with a 20-percentile point gain in student achievement" (Marzano, 2010, p. 71).

Specific benefits to understanding and performing mathematics through gaming are found in Table 6.1.

Table 6.1.   Benefits and Impact of Specific Game Attributes

Benefit	Instructional and Self-Efficacy Impact
Impact students' levels of self efficacy	Provide authentic opportunities for students to be influenced by effective mastery, verbal persuasion, and vicarious experiences.
Families involved in a positive approach to learning mathematics	Offer an enjoyable and effective way for parents to actively participate in their children's education. Students work on skills, watch others reason, work on basic facts or other procedures, and hear words of encouragement; Families can become more connected and supportive of classroom mathematics lessons taught and concepts/skills expected of their students.
Conceptual development of content	Game objectives require students' strategic thinking, reasoning, analyzing, and using information to win or work with others to problem solve.
Mathematics fact fluency improvement	Reinforce and help students recall whole number, decimal, and rational number basic facts and algorithmic procedures to win points for individual growth or team play.
Multiple Assessment Opportunities	Observing student reactions during game playing, student interviews, journals, surveys present a fuller assessment record.
Promote cooperative learning	Helping classmates reach a common goal provides practical reasons for cooperative learning and a context for verbal persuasion and vicarious experiences.
Address Common Core Standards of Practice	Provides practical application for making sense of problems, reasoning abstractly, using arguments and patterns to model concepts, and precise responses.
Differentiated instruction	Supports English language learners play and learn with objects and manipulatives, limiting language requirements to participate. Assign specific students to games designed to practice and understand content and skills targeted to a variety of ability levels and learning needs.

The following section describes several games focused on major topics of the K–8 curriculum. Each example is described for instructional use, purpose, needed materials, grade or age level, directions and variations. These games can be varied as needed for students' level of understanding and skill. These games are repeatable because of the element of chance in being presented with examples to solve. The games are classroom tested, applicable to a wide variety of student ability levels and address the benefits listed in Table 6.1. Most of the following games are played with wooden cubes on which numerals can be written. Blank wooden cubes can be found in discount stores, teachers' or craft stores and online for those sites. These games can be varied to match students' learning levels and mathematics curriculum. Students can work with families or in class rooms with these activities and find them both enjoyable and educational.

PLACE VALUE GAMES

Who Is in the Right Place?

- Purpose: This game provides practice for students to choose their own multi place numerals and identify by correct place value positions such as ones, tens, hundreds, thousands, et cetera.
- Group size: 1 to whole class
- Materials: Sets of blank index cards. One set of 10 cards is marked with a numeral 0–9 and the word "ones." Second set of 10 cards is marked with numerals 0–9 and the word "tens." Third set of 10 cards is marked with numerals 0–9 and the word "hundreds," and so on, depending on the number of digits students are told to write for their numeral.
- Example:

```
┌─────────────────┐
│        3        │
│                 │
│      TENS       │
└─────────────────┘
```

- Directions: Students write a 3, 4, or 5 digit numeral or more on each line of their paper. The leader draws a card and calls out the numeral and place indicated, such as "three tens." If the player has a "3" in the "ten place" in the numeral he/she created, the player circles the numeral. The winner is the first player to have all digits in one round circled. When that happens, the player calls out "Right Place."
- Example: if the first numeral written is 342, a player must have circled 3 in the hundreds, 4 in the tens and 2 in the ones places when those cards were called out. The leader keeps a record of cards called.
- A worksheet for this game is found in Appendix C.

ROUNDS

1. _____
2. _____
3. _____

Play the Place to Win

- Purpose: This game involves strategizing and estimating the size of numerals to choose so that their combination does not exceed the target number for the game. Players also practice addition of multidigit numerals and estimation.
- Materials: Game sheet, number cubes with digits from 0–9; one cube is marked 0–6, second cube is marked 4–9
- Group size: 2 to the whole class
- Directions: (1) Players decide upon a target number. (2) First player rolls the number cube and all players record the digit in only one column. A "0" is then recorded in any column to the right of that round. (3) Play continues as each player decides in which column to place the new rolled number until all rounds are played. (4) The winner is the player whose columns adds up to but does not exceed the target number. (5) Any number of columns can be played.
- Example: Target-500

Rounds	Hundreds	Tens	Ones
1		3	0
2	2	0	0
3	1	0	0
4		4	0
5		6	0
6			9
Total	4	3	9

- A blank playing board for this game is found in Appendix C.

Shape Game

- Purpose: Players place a numeral in different place value positions to form an addition, or subtraction, or multiplication, or division problem to find an answer to win the game. If the target of a round is to achieve the "highest sum" or "smallest product," for example, players place numerals in shapes, then use one of the four operations to make a problem with an answer that fits the highest or lowest target that was named.
- Group Size: 2 to whole class

- Materials: Paper shapes in which to write numerals, pencil or markers, number cubes marked with 0– 6 and 7, 8, 9, 1, 2, 3.
- Directions: (1) Players decide or choose an operation and whether the "highest" or "lowest" answer will win the round. Players are told the numerals that are on the cube to be tossed. (2) Leader tosses the cube. (3) Each player writes the called numeral in one shape of the problem and computes the operation. (4) Players win points by correctly computing highest or lowest answer in the class, depending on the agreed-upon goal for that round.
- Playing mat examples:

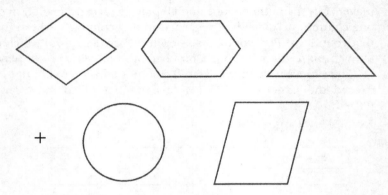

- A blank playing board for this game is found in Appendix C.

ADDITION, SUBTRACTION, MULTIPLICATION, AND DIVISION COMPUTATION GAMES

Add On

- Purpose: Players practice addition skills, including combinations that involve regrouping. Any numerals to be reinforced for addition can be placed in boxes by teacher or leader.
- Group size: Two:
- Materials: Game board, marker to move around board, Wooden cube or cards marked with letters: R-Right, L-Left, D- Down, N-lose a turn, C- move any way, U – up.
- Directions: (1) Players choose a "target" number to get to by adding the squares he/she lands on. (2) First player puts a counter on "FREE" and rolls cube. He/she moves counter as indicated by the cube. That is his/her first score. (3) Next player follows the same

steps as the first player and keeps the number landed on as a first score. (4) Play continues as each player moves his/her counter in the direction indicated by the cube and adds the number newly landed on to his/her score. (5) If a player lands above or below the grid, he/she loses a turn.

- The first player to get to the target number wins.
- Differentiation: Decimal numerals can be substituted for whole numbers. Decimal numerals can be substituted for whole number numerals. The size (2 or more digits) of numerals should be related to level of classroom instruction or practice needed
- A blank playing board for this game is found in Appendix C.

500 Shakedown

- Purpose: Players practice subtraction facts, including subtraction with borrowing or regrouping.
- Group Size: Two
- Materials: 2 wooden number cubes.* One is marked with 0–5 and the other is marked with 4–9 or commercial dice are used, paper and pencil for each player.
- Directions: (1) Each player starts with 500 points. Player #1 rolls 2 dice or number cubes and makes the largest two-digit number he/she can. (2) Player subtracts their number from 500. Example: Player #1 rolls a 2 and a 4 and makes 42. He/she subtracts 42 from 500. (3) Player #2 rolls the dice and subtracts their number from 500. Players continue to alternate turns. The first person to reach 0 wins. (4) If player rolls a "1," he/she must make the smallest two-digit number possible with cubes and add that numeral to the running score. Example: If the player throws a 1 and a 5, the smallest two-digit number is 15. He/she adds 15 to the total.
- Differentiation: Start with 5,000 or 500,000 points and use three or four dice.
- *Blank wooden cubes can be found in discount stores, teachers' or craft stores and online for those sites.
- A blank playing board for this game is found in Appendix C.

Crazy Mixed Up Numbers

- Purpose: Players learn to match groups of objects to a numeral, decide how many objects to join together or separate to make new groups, understand the meaning of addition and subtraction processes.
- Size of Groups: Two or whole class.
- Materials: Counters, number cubes or index cards marked with numerals from 0 – 20.
- Directions: (1) The object of the game is to identify the number of objects in a group and the number removed or joined to make a new group. (2) Player #1 reads a numeral from an index card or rolls a number cube to generate a numeral. (3) The rest of the players form a set of objects to match that numeral. (4) Player #1 calls out another numeral from cards or cubes. (5) The rest of the players then form the new set and tells player #1 how many counters were joined or removed to form the first set of objects to make the new set. (6) Play continues for six sets of making a group of objects, then adding or reducing it and reporting that amount. A new leader/player #1 is then chosen.
- Example: Player #1 calls out "10" from the cards or cubes.

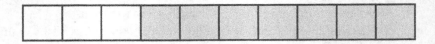

The other players make a group of 10 objects. Player #1 then calls out "3." The other players removes enough objects from their set of 10 to now see "3." Players then report "7" because 7 objects had to be removed to have 3 left.

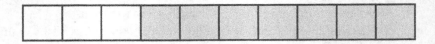

Later, student should record the number sentences formed with the manipulatives, such as $10 - 7 = 3$.

Multiplication Moves

- Purpose: Players strategize to choose numerals to multiply together. Players also strategize to form a multiplication combination that will result in 3 products in a row on the game board.
- Group Size: Two or more players
- Materials: Game board, markers to move, pen/pencil to write initials
- Directions: (1) The goal of the game is to form a horizontal, vertical or diagonal line of three products in a row. (2) The first player puts a counter on two different numerals above bold line at top of chart. The player then multiplies the 2 numerals and writes his/her initials in the box containing the product. (3) The second player moves just one of the two counters to designate a new pair of factors. One counter can be placed on the same numeral as the other counter. The factors are then multiplied and the new product is marked with the second student's initial. Each player tries to find products that will block the row of the other player's products. (4) The game continues until one player has found 3 products in a horizontal, vertical or diagonal row Example: Player #1 chooses "3" and "4" above the bold line and places a counter or marker on each numeral. Player than writes his/her initials in "12" on playing board. On the player's next turn, the counter on top of 3 or 4 is moved to make a new multiplication combination. If player moves the counter over from "4" to "5," because "15," is near the "12," the player multiplies 5 x 3. That player's initials are marked over "15" on the game board. Play continues to form combinations that are 3 in a row on game board.
- Differentiation: The factors in the bolded top row can include 10, 11, 12 and the products increased.
- A blank playing board for this game is found in Appendix C.

Salute Multiplication

- Purpose: Players practice multiplication facts and use reasoning to name the missing numerals.
- Group Size: 2 players
- Materials: Deck of cards with face cards removed, or index cards with numerals written on them from 0 – as high as teacher or leader chooses to relate to curriculum or provide opportunity for practice of any numerals.

- Directions: (1) Cards are shuffled and placed face down. (2) Player #1 turns over the top card and places it faces up on the table for all to see. (3) Player #2 draws a card without looking at it. (4) Player #2 holds the card above his or her eyes so that player #1 can see it, but player #2 cannot. (5) Player #1 multiplies the 2 cards mentally and says the product out loud. (6) Player #2 listens and decides what his or her card must be so that the product of the first card and unseen playing card is correct. Player #2 announces the value of the unseen card he/she chose. Example: Player #1 turns over a 6 for all to see. Without looking at it, player #2 puts a card with a "4" on his/her forehead. Player #1 mentally multiplies 6 x 4 and says, "24." Player #2 must respond with "4" because 6 x 4 = 24.
- Both players decide if the response is correct. If it is, player #1 gets 1 point.
- Players reverse roles and play continues until one player has 10 points.

Remainder Game

- Purpose: Players practice division facts, including combinations that have division remainders.
- Group size: Two or more players:
- Materials: Game Board, markers to move along board, one wooden cube with digits marked with 1–6, Second cube is marked 4–9.
- Directions: Players put their markers on "START" on game board. (1) The first player rolls a number cube and divides the numeral shown on the cube into the numeral in the START box on the game board. (2) Player then moves his/her marker the number of places that is the same as the remainder of division problem. If remainder is "0," player does not move marker. Example: First player rolls a 3. He/she divides 3 into 23 to get 7, remainder 2. The marker is moved 2 spaces and lands on "7." On the next turn, the player rolls the cube and gets "4." He/she divides 4 into 7 and gets a remainder of "3." He/she moves the marker 3 places from 7 and is now on "26." (3) Next player takes a turn. (4) Markers move in the directions of the arrows. The first player to move marker to HOME or past HOME, wins game. Sample of playing board:

29	46	54	12	8	HOME

26	15	9	7	2	START 23

- Blank wooden cubes can be found in discount stores, teachers' or craft stores and online for those sites.
- A blank playing board for this game is found in Appendix C.

FRACTION GAMES

Fraction Bingo

- Purpose: Practice naming equivalent fractions and/or mixed numbers.
- Group Size: four to five students.
- Materials:
  - 3x3 playing card with nine sections (sections contain fractions and/or mixed numbers)
  - Call cards containing different names (or pictures) for the fractional numbers on the playing mat
  - Disc or counters to cover numeral on play card
- Directions: (1) The game is played like bingo. A caller is chosen and holds up a card from the pile. (2). Any player, who has an equivalent fraction or mixed number covers the corresponding call with a disc. The first player to obtain three discs in a row (vertically, horizontally, or diagonally) is the winner.

- Call Card Example:

1/3		

- Sample Playing Mat

1/3	1/2	25/100
10/12	free	9/15
2/10	2/6	5/10

- A blank playing board for this game is found in Appendix C.

Fract Match

- Purpose: Recognize different number names that match.
- Group Size: 2 to 6
- Materials:
  - o Set of 3 x 5 inch cards with numerals for common fractions—1/2, 1/4. 2/3, 5/6, 7/8, 4/8—and any others with which students are working.
  - o Second set of cards that contains pictures of sets, regions, and line segments representing the fractions; Make more than one picture for each fraction card.

- Directions: (1) The dealer shuffles the fraction cards and puts them face down. He/she shuffles the picture cards and deals all of them. Each player puts his/her picture cards face down in a pile. (2) At the dealers' signal each player turns over his/her top card. If any one or more of the picture cards match the fraction card, the player says, "Fract match." The first player to say it gets all of the picture card that have been turned up. (3) Play continues with the dealer turning fraction cards and players turning picture cards until all the picture cards have been played. (When players turn over their last picture card without making a match with the top fraction card, each one shuffles his/her remaining cards and puts them face down again so they can continue to play). (4) The winner is the player who collects the most cards.

- Differentiation: Students can look at representations of fractions and write the fraction the picture represents. Example: Fraction and pictures.

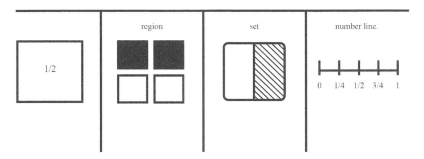

Add 'Em Up!

- Purpose: Players practice adding fractions.
- Group size: Two or more
- Materials: Two different colored number cubes marked with any single digits, except "0," paper and pencil for each player
- Directions: (1) Players decide which color cube will represent the numerator, and which color cube will represent the denominator. (2) The first player rolls the cubes, records the fraction rolled, and passes the cubes to the next player. Each player then records the fraction rolled. (3) After each player has a second turn, he/she will record the addition combination thrown. (4) The first player to reach or exceed an agreed upon whole number (such as 3) is the winner.

- Example:
  - ○ Target fraction: 1 1/12
  - ○ First round: Carl rolls 1/2
  - ○ Second round: Carl rolls 1/4 and now adds 1/2 to 1/4 for the score of 3/4.
  - ○ Third round: Carl rolls 2/6 and then adds 2/6 to 3/4 for a new total of 13/12 or 1 1/12
  - ○ Carl wins that round.
- Differentiation: Students can subtract, multiply or divide fractions.
- Score sheet is found in appendix C.

Fraction Concentration

- Purpose: Players practice finding fraction equivalences and writing fraction names word names.
- Group Size: groups of two students.
- Materials: 30 index cards, marked with 1/2, 1/3, 2/3, 1/4, 2/4, 3/4, 1/5, 2/5, 3/5, 4/5, 1/6, 2/6, 3/6, 4/6, 5/6 on 15 cards. The corresponding word names for the fractions are written on the other 15 cards.
- Directions: (1) Students play "concentration" using fractions and their corresponding word names. (2) All 30 cards are placed, blank side up, on a table in rows. (3) Students take turns turning over two cards at a time. If they match, the student keeps them. If the cards do not match, they are turned back over. Game ends when all cards are matched.

More or Less

- Purpose: Players practice fraction order, deciding which fraction is larger or smaller than another.
- Group Size: Two
- Materials: Index cards, each marked with different fractions.
- Directions: (1) Cards are shuffled and placed faced down. (2) For round one, a card is drawn by each player. (3) The player who draws the card with the greater fraction wins the other player's card. (4) The winner is the player who ends with the most cards.

Toss to Win With Shape Page

- Purpose: Players practice addition, subtraction, multiplication and division of fractions; players practice ordering fractions by deciding in which shape to put larger and smaller numbers.
- Group Size: 2 students or whole class
- Materials:
  - Game Sheets
  - Two number cubes. One is marked with "0", "1", "2", "3", "4", "5", and the second is marked with "5", "6", "7", "8", "9", "0".
- Directions: (1) The players decide which operation to use, addition, subtraction, multiplication or division, on the game sheet. (2) The players then decide, for the pattern chosen, if the goal for that computation should be highest or lowest correct answer. (3) The leader chooses which number cube to use for the tossing and tells the players which numerals are on that cube. (4) The leader then tosses the cube and players write the revealed numeral in one of the shapes in the chosen pattern. Once the numeral is recorded, it cannot be moved or erased. Only one numeral is recorded in one shape before the cube is rolled again. (5) Players compute the example. The player whose answer is either the highest or lowest answer in the class, depending on the target, wins the round.
- Example of patterns for addition round:

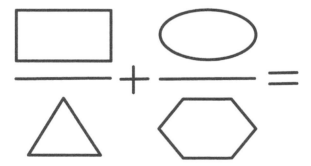

- Playing board can be found in Appendix C.

DECIMAL GAMES

How Much Is Your Word Worth?

- Purpose: Practice addition of decimal numerals
- Group size: 2 or more students
- Materials: Worksheet such as the following (numbers are cents each letter is worth), pencil/marker

a	b	c	d	e	f	g	h	I	j
.10	.20	.30	.40	.50	.60	.70	.80	.90	.01
k	l	m	n	o	p	q	r	s	y
.02	.03	.04	.05	.06	.07	.08	.09	1.10	1.11
u	v	w	x	y	z				
1.12	1.13	1.14	1.15	1.16	1.17				

- Directions: (1) Leader writes a word on the board and students calculate its worth. (2) Players should choose their own words for practice. Example: **smile**

$$
\begin{array}{rcl}
s & = & 1.10 \\
m & = & 0.04 \\
i & = & 0\ 90 \\
l & = & 0.03 \\
+\quad e & = & 0.50 \\
\hline
& \$ & 2.57
\end{array}
$$

- Differentiation: (1) Players could see how many $1.00 or more words they can find. (2) Change the numerical values for other games. (3) Use science and social studies words when possible. (4) Players can subtract, multiply or divide total of two words.
- Playing board can be found in Appendix C.

Ordering Decimals

- Purpose: Practice putting decimals in order—from lowest to highest
- Group size: 2 players
- Materials: Cut paper (or use index cards) into 20 sections and on each write one of these decimals: 0.1, 0.2, 0.3, 0.4, 0.5, 0.6, 0.7, 0.8, 0.9, 1.0, 1.10, 1.20, 1.30, 1.40, 1.50, 1.60, 1.70, 1.80, 1.90, 2.00

- Directions: (1) Each player is dealt 5 cards (sections) which are face up in the order they were received. The rest of the cards are face down in a pile. (2) The players draw from the deck or take the last discarded card. The new card can replace a player's card to help order or it can be discarded. A card being replaced is discarded. The first player to have his cards ordered from the lowest to the highest card calls out.
- Differentiation: Fractions can be used in place of decimals.

Choose Your Decimals!

- Purpose: Players practice decimal computation and use of operations.
- Group Size: Two or whole class
- Materials: Paper and pencil
- Directions: (1) Players draw shapes as seen in the example and choose a target number for a sum, difference, product or quotient. (2) Leader will make six draws from a box of cards with number 0 to 9 or roll a number cube. (3) Players write the numerals in any boxes, being allowed to skip 2 draws. (4) When first four boxes are filled, players place decimal points and + or – or x or ÷ anywhere between the boxes. All operation signs do not have to be used. A player could use the same operation or any combination. Also, boxes can be pushed to make a 2-digit number in the number sentence being created. The person closest to the target number wins.

$$\square \ \square \ \square \ \square = \square \ \square$$

- Differentiation:
  - Any arrangement of boxes will work, depending on difficulty of game.
  - Game can be played using only one operation or combination of operations.
  - Have students fill in single digit numerals without using operations.
  - Playing board can be found in Appendix C.

CONCLUSION

In a global sense, mathematics games, whether played on paper, on line, singly, in pairs or with a whole class, can offer learning and self-efficacy advantages to learners for several reasons. Research indicates that students develop higher levels of self-efficacy when actively engaged (enactive mastery), listening to their fellow students or family reason and make decisions to gain points (vicarious experiences) and hear encouragement as games are won or good moves are applauded (verbal persuasion). Variables of educational settings, precise game descriptors, and differences in teacher/student interactions prevent creating a definitive list of high quality games. Describing effective frameworks and game characteristics, rather than specific games, affect the attitude and content success. Mathematics education research has found and reported that student engagement is one of the strongest motivators for learning.

Games can extend learning to the home as families help their students reinforce classroom lessons with skills and reasoning practice. Games that are most effective and successful are clearly related and enhance classroom lessons, provide various levels of interest and content, support ELL learners and help students learn to communicate. As students engage in games that are fun and motivating, students can more easily accept that they are, indeed, "a math person."

Games add the element of enjoyment to learning mathematics content and processes in a context encouraging self-efficacy that impacts students' beliefs in their ability to succeed. The important element of paper/pencil games or those played on a computer make the experience interesting, fun, appealing, and supportive of students' confidence in their own success.

DISCUSSION QUESTIONS

1. As a teacher, parent or observer, what do you suggest are the characteristics you identify for a successful and appealing game?
2. What do games offer to students in order to increase confidence in learners' own math ability?
3. Did you play mathematics games in your own schooling? If so, which do you recall and why are them memorable?
4. Why do you think there is an increased interest in gaming in mathematics classrooms?
5. How could you respond to a teacher who is not using games because of the time they take to prepare or for student organization issues?

6. Why do you think many people have a less than satisfactory level of self-efficacy in understanding and using mathematics? What types of games or which game characteristics could improve those beliefs?

REFERENCES

Afari, E., Algridge, J., & Fraser, B. (2012). Effectiveness of using games in tertiary level mathematics classrooms. *International Journal of Science and Mathematics Education, 10*(6), 1369–1392.

Franklin, S, Peat, M, & Lewis, A. (2003). A non-traditional interventions to stimulate discussion: The use of games and puzzles. *Journal of Biological Education, 37*(2), 79–84.

Hays, R. T. (2005). The effectiveness of instructional games. A literature review and discussion (Technical Report 2005-004). Naval Air Warfare Center Training Systems Division. Retrieved from https://www.silversprite.com/?p=2601

Ke, F., & Grabowski, B. (2007). Gameplaying for maths learning: Cooperative or not? *British Journal of Educational Technology, 38*(2), 249–259. doi:10.1111/j.1467-8535.2006.00593.x

Mathematics Learning Study Committee. (2001). *Adding it up: Helping children learn mathematics* (J. Kilpatrick, J. Swafford, & B. Findell, Eds.). Washington, DC: National Academy Press

Marzano, R. J. (2010). Using games to enhance student achievement. *Meeting Students Where They Are, 67,* 71–72.

MacKenty, B. (2006). All play and no work. *School Library Journal, 52,* 46–48.

Opolot-Okurut, C. (2010). Classroom learning environment and motivation towards mathematics among secondary school students in Uganda. *Learning Environments Research, 13,* 267–277. doi:10.1007/s10984-010-9074-7

Ross, J., & Bruce, C. (2007). Professional development effects on teacher efficacy: Results o randomized field trial. *The Journal of Educational Research, 101*(1), 50–60. doi:10.3200/JOER.101.1.50-60

Rutherford, K (2015). *Why play math games? Teaching children mathematics,* Reston, VA: National Council of Teachers of Mathematics.

Schrand, T. (2008). Tapping into active learning and multiple intelligences with interactive multimedia: A low-threshold classroom approach. *College Teaching, 56*(2): 78–84.

Sherman, H., Richardson, L., & Yard, G. (2019). *Teaching learners who struggle with mathematics: Reasoning with systematics intermention and remediations* (4th ed.). Long Grove, IL: Pearson Education

Vandercruysse, S., Vandewaetere, M., & Clarebout, G. (2012). Game based learning: A review on the effectiveness of educational games. Retrieved July 1, 2018 from https://www.researchgate.net/publication/260360868_Game-Based_Learning_A_Review_on_the_Effectiveness_of_Educational_Games

CHAPTER 7

PULLING IT ALL TOGETHER

Self-Efficacy in Math, Lifelong Learning, and the Importance of Parents and Teachers in Shaping Student-Confidence

This book examined Albert Bandura's (1977a, 1977b, 1982a, 1982b, 1986, 1997) social learning theory and self-efficacy theory applications toward educating elementary and middle school students in mathematics. The dominate goal of this book was to inform teachers and families of the value of enhancing their students' levels of self-efficacy, and providing strategies for doing so. An additional goal was to sensitize teachers to their own levels of self-efficacy, factors that influenced their efficacy, and to guide them toward productive relationships with colleagues, administrators, and parents through a self-efficacy lens.

Recall from Chapter 1 that social learning theory posits that thoughts, actions, and the environment all interact with each other to inform individuals of possible behaviors in any given context. No behavior is possible—whether it be trying a new teaching method, or beginning homework on a difficult assignment—without first a thought, an assessment of one's ability to perform the task, and an assessment of the environmental response for doing it (e.g., a reward or punishment). As part of social learning theory, self-efficacy theory posits that one's willingness to engage in a behavior—especially a new behavior—is judged, first, by a

Learning Mathematics Successfully: Raising Self-Efficacy in Students, Teachers, and Parents
pp. 147–155
Copyright © 2019 by Information Age Publishing
All rights of reproduction in any form reserved.

belief in the ability to successfully perform the behavior and, second, if performed, by a belief that it will lead to a desired outcome. We examined how these principles transcended age and roles and applied equally to mathematics students, teachers, and parents alike.

The activities and examples provided in this book relate directly to the four primary sources of self-efficacy information, listed here in order of influence:

- **Enactive Mastery.**   Creating opportunities for a person to *perform* the desired behavior. The belief that one can successfully perform a behavior increases as one has the opportunity to perform it correctly, even if under guidance and monitoring initially.
- **Vicarious Experiences.**   Watching others perform the behavior successfully. If I am attempting a new behavior, my confidence in performing it successfully is increased if I can watch someone with my novice skill level perform it.
- **Verbal Persuasion.**   Having a person of influence—a teacher or parent—express confidence in one's ability to perform a behavior can influence a student whether or not to even try. While not as powerful as allowing them to actually perform the behavior, or watching someone else perform it, it can be an important adjunct to the previous two in giving students the confidence to try.
- **Physiological States.**   Our bodies send us confidence cues in the form of sweating palms, shallow breathing, or a racing heartbeat. These physiological triggers can paralyze a student in fear. A relaxed environment (e.g., it's okay to fail—just try it) can abort these physiological cues of fear and enable students to feel calmer about trying a new skill.

Table 7.1 identifies some questions teachers can ask themselves about how they are addressing these four critical sources of information when planning activities for students, parents, and even themselves.

Being sensitive to students', parents', and even your own level of self-efficacy, may be new for some teachers. In addition, being sensitive to the four sources of information and planning a teaching style that maximizes self-efficacy in students can require patience, practice, and perhaps a reconceptualization of the teachers' and parents' roles. These types of changes require time and practice as well as a commitment among the larger faculty. While some of the ideas and strategies presented in this book may seem idealistic in some instances, they rank among the best practices toward which teachers should strive.

Table 7.1. Planning for the Four
Critical Sources of Self-Efficacy Information

Efficacy Source	For Students	For Teachers	For Parents
Enactive mastery	What opportunities am I planning for students to perform?	Am I provided a chance to "try out" new teaching behaviors and instructional methods in a safe/practicing environment first?	What is it I would like parents to *do*? Can they role-play with me strategies I recommend?
Vicarious experiences	How can I plan for students to watch others perform the mathematics operation successfully?	Do I have opportunities to watch master-teachers perform the new skills requested of me?	What opportunities exist for parents to see good parenting in action? How can I facilitate this?
Verbal persuasion	Do I provide enough verbal confidence in my students?	Do we, as a faculty, give each other encouragement for trying new skills?	What are my communications with parents like? Do I express enough confidence and appreciation of them?
Physiological states	How do I make my classroom environment stress-free and accepting of initial failure?	Do I understand what makes me nervous? Do I know how to calm my own nerves in stressful situations?	How do parents behave when talking with me? Calm and relaxed, or fidgety or nervous? What can I do to put them at ease?

Highly efficacious mathematics teachers learn how to create activities that enable student mastery and instill in their students a belief that, with adequate effort, the student can successfully complete advanced math courses. For example, Chapter 6 provided examples of how self-efficacy is raised when students engage in gaming activities. These activities provide enjoyable and interesting opportunities to be impacted by enactive mastery, verbal persuasion, and vicarious experiences.

Highly efficacious mathematics teachers also attend to their own skill-building through professional development and being aware of teacher research. In addition to these things, they realize exactly how much they (and parents) are role-model examples to students and model for students problem-solving skills in an efficacious way. On a broader level, they realize that the self-efficacy skills they instill in their students generalize to other academic areas, and hopefully create lifelong learners who are set to meet whatever challenges await in adulthood. How, exactly, are teachers and parents role models in self-efficacy for their students, and how does an early grounding in self-efficacy position a student for success in advanced coursework and life?

Teachers and Parents as Self-Efficacy Models.   Students spend the vast part of their waking hours in the presence of a teacher or guardian. As such, these two groups are in uniquely powerful positions to model problem-solving behaviors for students which is another form of "vicarious experiences"—the second most important influence of self-efficacy. Teachers and parents, by their intimate relationships with students, also hold a powerful influence over what is *said* to students—self-efficacy's third most important influence of "verbal persuasion." Thus, coupled with opportunities for students to perform these behaviors themselves, teachers and parents control the top three influences of self-efficacy.

Let us look at a few examples of how this could work. Teachers and parents go through the day making decisions and problem-solving. How can some of these decisions be shared with students so that they can observe problem-solving in action? One middle school math teacher decided to share with her class her decision about buying and financing a new car by turning the experience into a word problem for the class to help solve:

> I found a car to buy that costs $25,000. I need to figure out the best payment options so I pay as little for this car as possible. My options are:
>
> - I could pay cash, but then I lose 4% interest that I'm earning on the $25,000.
> - I could pay $5,000 down and then finance the remaining $20,000 at 5% interest for 4 years.
> - I could pay $10,000 down and finance the remaining $15,000 at 3% interest for 4 years.
>
> In which scenario do I pay the least amount of money? How do I figure this out?"

Parents also have opportunities to bring their child into problem-solving decisions. One father needed to hook up a new piece of technology in the home. He decided to share his learning experience with his child, "I'm not sure how to do this as I've never done it, but I'll figure it out." He then explained that his first step would be read the instructions and attempt to connect it and then test it. If that failed, he would go online and see if anyone else experienced problems. He also said he could ask the next door neighbor for help if he needed to as that family had the same device. This simple conversation conveyed several key examples:

- I can do this and will eventually figure it out one way or another
- I will read and follow directions

- It's alright to ask for outside help if I get stuck

These types of student inclusion in problems and decisions may not be self-evident for parents—or even teachers. As part of coaching parents, teachers can offer suggestions on how to serve as poignant examples of self-efficacious behavior. Knowing that influential adults do not have all the answers, and need to problem-solve. can be an important "teachable moment" for students and serve as an example for them to copy the behavior (and can-do attitude) required to solve a problem and seek solutions.

The other critically important role teachers and parents play in developing an efficacious mindset in students is what is said to them—Verbal Persuasion. Tied into this concept are theories of intelligence that are wittingly (or unwittingly) passed along to students—theories the students internalize. One theory of intelligence is *fixed intelligence*—the idea that ability is genetic and there is not much a person can do about it. If students adopt this theory, they do not believe they possess the basic ability to understand mathematics and will never be good at it. It provides a convenient excuse for not trying—and eventually failing. Some parents, in an attempt to commiserate with a frustrated or struggling child, will echo this theory by saying "I know—I'm not a 'math person' either." The other theory, *malleable intelligence,* posits that effort and persistence are far more important to success than innate ability. Those possessing a malleable intelligence perspective will believe they can find solutions to problems with adequate preparation and effort.

Educational psychologists believe that mathematical intelligence is more malleable than fixed, with most estimating that only 40–45% of mathematical variance is explained by innate ability—leaving over half of the variance explained by effort and persistence. This does not mean that any student can become an Albert Einstein, Stephen Hawking, or Ada Lovelace, who was the first computer programmer. But, it does mean that students can master elementary, middle and secondary math with coaching and effort.

Teachers and parents who adopt a malleable intelligence perspective, and strive to impart that perspective on their students, generally convey to students three principles (Deans for Impact, 2015):

- They know students are more motivated if they believe intelligence and ability can be improved with hard work.
- They praise students' productive efforts and strategies—and other factors under the students' control—rather than their ability.

- Teacher and parents help students feel more in control by helping them focus on learning goals (goals for improvement) rather than performance goals (e.g., goals for approval).

Blackwell, Trzesniewski, and Dweck (2007) tested these principles in a randomized study of middle school math students and found that those experiencing teachers with a malleable-intelligence approach to mathematics scored higher on assignments, had more positive beliefs about effort, and accurately attributed their grade to effort and strategies over those in the fixed-intelligence control group. In a simultaneous second study, declining grades and attitudes were reversed in a randomized experiment with middle school students in which teachers adopted a malleable-intelligence approach to teaching mathematics.

The idea of "praising effort, not ability" is not new but it must be handled carefully. If a student tries hard, but fails, it is an empty consolation prize to say "Well, you tried hard—you get an A for effort!" That "A" does not translate into a reportable grade, and the teacher and student both know the result was failure. Instead of heaping empty praise on a struggling student, the teacher (and student) is best served by an honest assessment of why the failure occurred. Instead of empty praise, a more reasonable statement to the student might be: "I know you worked hard on this, and put a lot of time into it. Let's see where you went wrong and figure it out so you know next time." This acknowledges the obvious effort and time by the student, but also acknowledges that the result was not success. It also conveys that mistakes can be found and corrected and it becomes a learning experience for the student, rather than a confirmation that the student is a failure or "not a math person."

Teachers and parents need to be united in these messages for students because either parents or teachers can torpedo effective verbal messages of the other. Getting parents on the same page can be done in parent-teacher conferences, or even a simple note home to students' parents explaining the philosophy of the classroom with respect to learning mathematics. Helping parents reinforce your views that their student can learn mathematics, and can successfully complete the requirements of the course, avoids counterproductive mixed messages a student might hear. Parents can help teachers (and ultimately their student) in this goal by emphasizing goal setting, and emphasizing that success is the reward for effort, persistence, preparation and strategies. Parents can help by being examples, themselves, of effort and problem-solving persistence. Lastly, parents can help by adopting more of a malleable intelligence mindset themselves, and not try to rationalize failure in math as a result of genetics. Working together, teachers and parents can instill in students a belief system whereby results are tied to effort and persistence, and that all requirements for a given mathematics course can be successfully accomplished with hard work, rather than luck or ability.

Generalizing Self-Efficacy to Other Academic Areas.   The utility of self-efficacy theory would be severely compromised if it only contributed to one subject area, or in one classroom. Having students feel confident and proficient in math, only to have them stumble and remain unsure and scared of science, language arts, and other subjects would be counterproductive to most schools, and certainly the sign of a weak theory. Self-efficacy, however, is robust in that the principles underlying it can easily generalize to other subjects and situations (Bandura, 1997). Approaching problems in chemistry or biology is similar to approaching problems in algebra. Recall that self-efficacy is a process, and a mindset of believing in one's ability to perform tasks. While the process of performing academic tasks varies by individual, it usually requires a sequential organization of steps as well as a reliance on previously learned subskills. The acquired knowledge of these steps and skills provides the beliefs that one can successfully perform a task. In mathematics, it might be the operational rules of algebra and knowing addition, subtraction and multiplication. In reading Shakespeare, it might require a different set of rules and subskills. In dissecting a frog in biology, yet another set of operations and procedures. Students will not have the same level of skill development and organization of processes among subjects. Backgrounds in some subjects will be stronger than others, and cultivation of expertise will also necessarily be driven by personal interests.

This principle of learning new (or advanced) subjects by relying on organizational steps and knowledge of subskills is analogous to the call of educational psychologists to tie new knowledge and problem-solving to a knowledge of the problem's context and understanding of the problem's underlying structure (Deans for Impact, 2015). This can be done with strategic examples provided by the teacher. For example, calculating the area of the merry-go-round at the school picnic applies the same operations as calculating the area of a 16-inch pizza. In addition, alternating everyday examples (in word problems) with more abstract examples (i.e., mathematical formulas) helps students understand the underlying structure and relevancy of mathematical principles.

Another method for helping to generalize self-efficacy to other subjects is having teachers in other subject areas mimic each other's teaching and self-efficacy enhancing strategies. Evidence suggests that infusing self-efficacy enhancing strategies in diverse subjects (e.g., mathematics and language arts) helps reinforce not only the strategies for those two subjects, but can generalize to other unrelated subjects (Bandura, 1997). This is accomplished by creating a meta-cognition, or an awareness of what one knows and does not know. It also creates a mental system by which an individual plans problem-solving strategies consistent with the task at hand. Thus, it does not matter whether one is proficient in a subject, or particularly enjoys it. The level of one's self-efficacy determines the effort and confidence a student will expend to accomplish the assignment.

Self-Efficacy for Lifelong Learning and Meeting Life Challenges Into Adulthood. R. Buckminster Fuller's famous Doubling Learning Curve pointed out that, in 1900, knowledge doubled every century. By 1945, knowledge doubled every 25 years, and by 1982, every 12–13 months. IBM recently projected that, by 2020, knowledge could double in nano-technology sectors every 11–12 *hours.* Jeannie Meister, a contributor for *Forbes* magazine recently predicted that 91% of Millennial (defined as being born between 1977–1997) would stay in a job for less than 3 years, equating to between 15 and 20 jobs during one's lifetime. This explosive growth in knowledge, coupled with a corresponding rise in skills neces-sary to perform current and future jobs, means that our students will need to continually learn and acquire new skills beyond the knowledge and skills taught in today's K–12 schools. As students who are in elementary school now can be reasonably expected to be productive citizens into the 22nd century, we must equip them with the tools needed to adapt and change in response to an evolving world and workforce. We can no longer rely on our curriculum to sustain them throughout their working careers. What we *can* do, though, is equip them with the tools and skills needed to adapt to those changes.

Self-efficacious students will be able to more easily adapt to these changes. By providing skills in goal setting, awareness of strengths and weaknesses, tying success to effort and persistence, and valuing learning for learning's sake, we position our students to become self-directed life-long learners empowered to meet whatever cerebral challenges lay ahead and whatever their future workforce or career demands of them.

Possessing self-efficacy does even more than enable lifelong learning, and adapting to career changes. It provides skills to deal with personal life challenges, such as phobias, dysfunctional relationships, and physical rehabilitation that is sometimes needed as we age. Learning self-efficacy in elementary school—or at any stage of life—can mushroom into a life-long set of skills. Becoming self-efficacious in a unit on dividing fractions, for example, can establish a mindset of belief that, with effort and per-sistence, problems can be solved. This can, and will, generalize to increas-ingly difficult subjects and become established across a broader range of skills as students mature. By adulthood, we hope that students will gener-alize these skills into all areas of their adulthood, including breaking bad habits, solving (or at least addressing) relationship issues, and even confi-dently battling serious diseases. We provide math students with more than rules of operation and rote procedures—we provide them with a powerful tool that empowers them to thrive throughout their lives.

DISCUSSION QUESTIONS

1.   Given the content of this book, what are the 5 most important take-aways for you?
2.   How do you see yourself changing your professional practice on the basis of this book?
3.   What are some strategies you can use to enlist the cooperation of colleagues and parents into your efforts?
4.   What is the biggest challenge for you to incorporate the strategies discussed in this book?
5.   What is your first step?

REFERENCES

Bandura, A. (1977a). *Social learning theory*. Englewood Cliffs, NJ: Prentice-Hall.

Bandura, A. (1977b). Self-efficacy: Toward a unifying theory of behavior change. *Psychological Review, 84*(2), 191–215.

Bandura, A. (1982a). The assessment and predictive generality of self-percepts of efficacy. *Behavioral Therapy and Experimental Psychiatry, 13*(3), 195–199.

Bandura, A. (1982b). Self-efficacy mechanism in human agency. *American Psychologist, 37*(2), 122–147.

Bandura, A. (1986). *Social foundations of thought and action: A social cognitive theory*. Englewood Cliffs, NJ: Prentice-Hall.

Bandura, A. (1997). *Self-efficacy: The exercise of control*. New York, NY: W. H. Freeman and Company.

Blackwell, L. S., Trzesniewski, K. H., & Dweck, S. C. (2007). Implicit theories of intelligence predict achievement across adolescent transition: A longitudinal study and an intervention. *Child Development, 78*(1), 246–263.

Deans for Impact. (2015). *The science of learning*. Austin, TX: Author.

CHAPTER 8

APPENDIX A

TEACHER SELF-EFFICACY SCALES

Learning Mathematics Successfully: Raising Self-Efficacy in Students, Teachers, and Parents
pp. 157–160
Copyright © 2019 by Information Age Publishing

Teacher Beliefs - TSES

This questionnaire is designed to help us gain a better understanding of the kinds of things that create challenges for teachers. Your answers are confidential.

Directions: Please indicate your opinion about each of the questions below by marking any one of the nine responses in the columns on the right side, ranging from (1) "None at all" to (9) "A Great Deal" as each represents a degree on the continuum.

Please respond to each of the questions by considering the combination of your *current* ability, resources, and opportunity to do each of the following in your present position.

	None at all	Very Little	Some Degree	Quite A Bit	A Great Deal

1. How much can you do to get through to the most difficult students? ① ② ③ ④ ⑤ ⑥ ⑦ ⑧ ⑨
2. How much can you do to help your students think critically? ① ② ③ ④ ⑤ ⑥ ⑦ ⑧ ⑨
3. How much can you do to control disruptive behavior in the classroom? ① ② ③ ④ ⑤ ⑥ ⑦ ⑧ ⑨
4. How much can you do to motivate students who show low interest in school work? ① ② ③ ④ ⑤ ⑥ ⑦ ⑧ ⑨
5. To what extent can you make your expectations clear about student behavior? ① ② ③ ④ ⑤ ⑥ ⑦ ⑧ ⑨
6. How much can you do to get students to believe they can do well in school work? ① ② ③ ④ ⑤ ⑥ ⑦ ⑧ ⑨
7. How well can you respond to difficult questions from your students? ① ② ③ ④ ⑤ ⑥ ⑦ ⑧ ⑨
8. How well can you establish routines to keep activities running smoothly? ① ② ③ ④ ⑤ ⑥ ⑦ ⑧ ⑨
9. How much can you do to help your students value learning? ① ② ③ ④ ⑤ ⑥ ⑦ ⑧ ⑨
10. How much can you gauge student comprehension of what you have taught? ① ② ③ ④ ⑤ ⑥ ⑦ ⑧ ⑨
11. To what extent can you craft good questions for your students? ① ② ③ ④ ⑤ ⑥ ⑦ ⑧ ⑨
12. How much can you do to foster student creativity? ① ② ③ ④ ⑤ ⑥ ⑦ ⑧ ⑨
13. How much can you do to get children to follow classroom rules? ① ② ③ ④ ⑤ ⑥ ⑦ ⑧ ⑨
14. How much can you do to improve the understanding of a student who is failing? ① ② ③ ④ ⑤ ⑥ ⑦ ⑧ ⑨
15. How much can you do to calm a student who is disruptive or noisy? ① ② ③ ④ ⑤ ⑥ ⑦ ⑧ ⑨
16. How well can you establish a classroom management system with each group of students? ① ② ③ ④ ⑤ ⑥ ⑦ ⑧ ⑨
17. How much can you do to adjust your lessons to the proper level for individual students? ① ② ③ ④ ⑤ ⑥ ⑦ ⑧ ⑨
18. How much can you use a variety of assessment strategies? ① ② ③ ④ ⑤ ⑥ ⑦ ⑧ ⑨
19. How well can you keep a few problem students form ruining an entire lesson? ① ② ③ ④ ⑤ ⑥ ⑦ ⑧ ⑨
20. To what extent can you provide an alternative explanation or example when students are confused? ① ② ③ ④ ⑤ ⑥ ⑦ ⑧ ⑨
21. How well can you respond to defiant students? ① ② ③ ④ ⑤ ⑥ ⑦ ⑧ ⑨
22. How much can you assist families in helping their children do well in school? ① ② ③ ④ ⑤ ⑥ ⑦ ⑧ ⑨
23. How well can you implement alternative strategies in your classroom? ① ② ③ ④ ⑤ ⑥ ⑦ ⑧ ⑨
24. How well can you provide appropriate challenges for very capable students? ① ② ③ ④ ⑤ ⑥ ⑦ ⑧ ⑨

Teacher Beliefs

This questionnaire is designed to help us gain a better understanding of the kinds of things that create challenges for teachers. Your answers are confidential.

Directions: Please indicate your opinion about each of the questions below by marking any one of the nine responses in the columns on the right side, ranging from (1) "None at all" to (9) "A Great Deal" as each represents a degree on the continuum.

Please respond to each of the questions by considering the combination of your *current* ability, resources, and opportunity to do each of the following in your present position.

	None at all	Very Little	Some Degree	Quite A Bit	A Great Deal
1. How much can you do to control disruptive behavior in the classroom?	① ②	③ ④	⑤ ⑥	⑦ ⑧	⑨
2. How much can you do to motivate students who show low interest in school work?	① ②	③ ④	⑤ ⑥	⑦ ⑧	⑨
3. How much can you do to calm a student who is disruptive or noisy?	① ②	③ ④	⑤ ⑥	⑦ ⑧	⑨
4. How much can you do to help your students value learning?	① ②	③ ④	⑤ ⑥	⑦ ⑧	⑨
5. To what extent can you craft good questions for your students?	① ②	③ ④	⑤ ⑥	⑦ ⑧	⑨
6. How much can you do to get children to follow classroom rules?	① ②	③ ④	⑤ ⑥	⑦ ⑧	⑨
7. How much can you do to get students to believe they can do well in school work?	① ②	③ ④	⑤ ⑥	⑦ ⑧	⑨
8. How well can you establish a classroom management system with each group of students?	① ②	③ ④	⑤ ⑥	⑦ ⑧	⑨
9. To what extent can you use a variety of assessment strategies?	① ②	③ ④	⑤ ⑥	⑦ ⑧	⑨
10. To what extent can you provide an alternative explanation or example when students are confused?	① ②	③ ④	⑤ ⑥	⑦ ⑧	⑨
11. How much can you assist families in helping their children do well in school?	① ②	③ ④	⑤ ⑥	⑦ ⑧	⑨
12. How well can you implement alternative teaching strategies in your classroom?	① ②	③ ④	⑤ ⑥	⑦ ⑧	⑨

13. What is your gender?
    O Male
    O Female

14. What is your racial identity?
    O African American
    O White, Non-Hispanic
    O Other

15. What subject matter do you teach? (as many as apply)
    O All (Elementary/ Self-contained)
    O Math
    O Science
    O Language Arts
    O Social Studies

16. What level do you teach?
    O Elementary
    O Middle
    O High

17. What is the context of your school?
    O Urban
    O Suburban
    O Rural

18. What is the approximate proportion of students who receive free and reduced lunches at your school?
    O 0-20%
    O 21-40%
    O 41-60%
    O 61-80%
    O 81-100%

19. What grade level(s) do you teach?   Ⓚ ① ② ③ ④ ⑤ ⑥ ⑦ ⑧ ⑨

20. How many years have you taught?   ⓪ ① ② ③ ④ ⑤ ⑥ ⑦ ⑧ ⑨
   ⓪ ① ② ③ ④ ⑤ ⑥ ⑦ ⑧ ⑨

For office use only.
⓪ ① ② ③ ④ ⑤ ⑥ ⑦ ⑧ ⑨
⓪ ① ② ③ ④ ⑤ ⑥ ⑦ ⑧ ⑨
⓪ ① ② ③ ④ ⑤ ⑥ ⑦ ⑧ ⑨

Directions for Scoring the Teachers' Sense of Efficacy Scale

Developers: Megan Tschannen-Moran, College of William and Mary
                            Anita Wookfolk Hoy, the Ohio State University

Construct Validity

For information about the construct validity of the Teachers' Sense of Teacher Efficacy Scale, see:

> Tschannen-Moran, M. & Woolfolk Hoy, A.W. (2001). Teacher efficacy: Capturing an elusive construct. *Teaching and Teacher Education, 17,* 783-805, https://doi.org/10.1016/S0742-051X(01)00036-1.

Factor Analysis

As we have used factor analysis to test this instrument, we have consistently found three moderately correlated factors: *Efficacy in Student Engagement, Efficacy in Instructional Practices,* and *Efficacy in Classroom Management.* At times, however, the make-up of the scales may vary slightly. With preservice teachers we recommend that the full scale (either 24-item or 12-item short form) be used, because the factor structure often is less distinct for these respondents.

Subscale Scores

To determine the *Efficacy in Student Engagement, Efficacy in Instructional Practices,* and *Efficacy in Classroom Management* subscale scores, we compute unweighted means of the items that load on each factor. Generally these groupings are:

Short Form		
Efficacy in Student Engagement	Items	2, 4, 7, 11
Efficacy in Instructional Strategies	Items	5, 9, 10, 12
Efficacy in Classroom Management	Items	1, 3, 6, 8
Long Form		
Efficacy in Student Engagement	Items	1, 2, 4, 6, 9, 12, 14, 22
Efficacy in Instructional Strategies	Items	7, 10, 11, 17, 18, 20, 23, 24
Efficacy in Classroom Management	Items	3, 5, 8, 13, 15, 16, 19, 21

Reliabilities

In the study reported in Tschaqnnen-Moran & Woolfolk Hoy (2001) above, the following reliabilities were found:

	Long Form			**Short Form**		
	Mean	SD	alpha	Mean	SD	alpha
TESE	7.1	.94	.94	7.1	.98	.90
Engagement	7.3	1.1	.87	7.2	1.2	.81
Instruction	7.3	1.1	.91	7.3	1.2	.86
Management	6.7	1.1	.90	6.7	1.2	.86

[1]Because this instrument was developed at the Ohio State University, it is sometimes referred to as the *Ohio State Teacher Efficacy Scale.* The developers prefer the name, *Teachers' Sense of Efficacy Scale.*

The interested reader can find a copy of the measure and scoring directions at http://wmpeople.wm.edu/site/page/mxtsch.

Scales and scoring guide used with permission.

CHAPTER 9

APPENDIX B

Parental Self-Efficacy Scale

Learning Mathematics Successfully: Raising Self-Efficacy in Students, Teachers, and Parents
pp. 161–162
Copyright © 2019 by Information Age Publishing

Parental Self-Efficacy Scale

Please indicate how strongly you agree or disagree with the following items	Strongly Disagree	Disagree	Slightly Disagree	Slightly Agree	Agree	Strongly Agree
I believe that I can help my child with their schoolwork.						
I believe that I can instill in my child the value of education.						
I believe that I can guide my child to avoid disciplinary problems.						
When my child experiences academic difficulties, I know how to guide them through it.						
If I need to, I know how to effectively deal with the teacher and/or school to solve problems.						
I know when to step in, and when to back off in helping my child with schoolwork.						
I know how to draw the connection between success in school and success in life for my child.						
If I am confused or do not know how to handle a parenting issue, I know who to contact for help.						
I am familiar with my child's lessons and know how to help if needed.						
I can prevent my child from falling under the influence of the wrong crowd.						

This scale is designed as either an inventory for parents to consider when reflecting on their parental abilities, or as a point of conversation between parent and teacher so that the teacher can help the parent address areas of perceived-weaknesses.

Other items can be added to the scale by either parents or teachers that are relevant to the population served. The purpose of this scale is not to achieve statistical data as much as it is to help parents think about areas they feel particularly strong and vulnerable in their parenting role.

CHAPTER 10

APPENDIX C

Game Board Templates

Learning Mathematics Successfully: Raising Self-Efficacy in Students, Teachers, and Parents
pp. 163–175
Copyright © 2019 by Information Age Publishing
All rights of reproduction in any form reserved.

Add 'Em Up

ROUNDS	PLAYER 1	PLAYER 2
1.		
2.		
3.		
4.		
	Total:	Total:

Add-On

				FREE				

R-RightL-Left   D-Down   N-Lose a turn   C-Move any way   U-Up

Choose Your Decimals

Rounds

1.

2.

3.

4.

Fraction Bingo

B	I	N	G	O
		FREE		

How Much is Your Word Worth?

A	B	C	D	E
F	G	H	I	J
K	L	M	N	O
P	Q	R	S	T
U	V	W	X	Y
Z				

Multiplication Moves

0	1	2	3	4	5	6	7	8	9
40	32	20	18	27	12	16	5	28	0
49	64	14	3	7	25	56	18	78	21
44	36	42	25	48	6	32	1	18	72
15	45	54	24	35	49	12	48	5	8
49	36	2	45	63	14	81	24	0	64
56	12	72	4	63	54	8	24	36	10
35	30	25	12	42	32	27	9	28	18
10	20	16	30	12	54	72	8	16	24

Play the Place to Win

Rounds	Thousands	Hundreds	Tens	Ones
1				
2				
3				
4				
5				
Total				

Choose Your Decimals

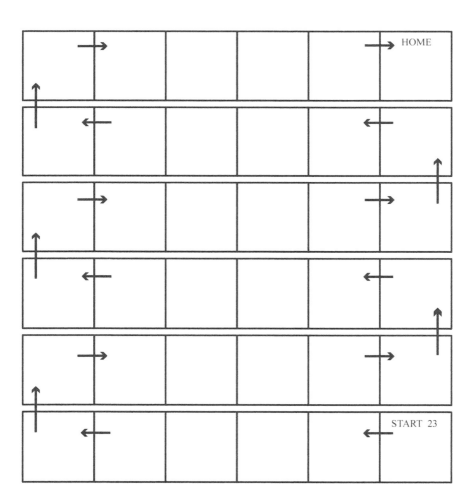

Who is in the Right Place?

<u>ROUNDS</u>

1._____

2._____

3._____

4._____

5._____

6._____

Shapes Game

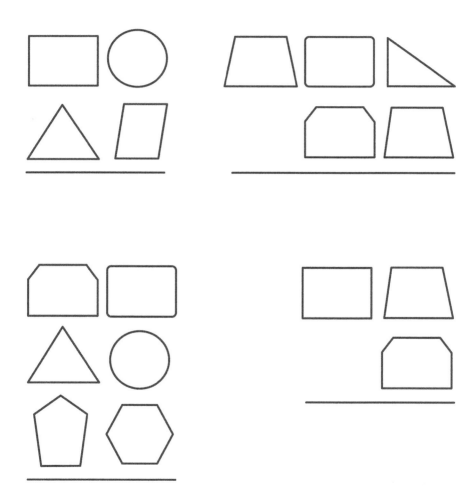

Choose Your Decimals

500 Shakedown

Player 1	Player 2	Player 3	Player 4
500 — _____	500 — _____	500 — _____	500 — _____
Difference:	Difference:	Difference:	Difference:

CHAPTER 11

APPENDIX D

Mathematics Games/Activities Websites

These websites provide standards-based math curricula, practice activities and games, assessment tools and instructive insights, and professional development.

Aleks
https://www.aleks.com
A web-based assessment and learning system that uses adaptive questioning to determine students' needs. It also instructs students on topics they are most ready to learn.
Grades: 3–12
Cost: $

Buzz Math
https://www.buzzmath.com
BuzzMath focuses on helping middle schoolers practice their math skills. It contains high-quality problems. It gives immediate and detailed feedback, letting students progress at their own pace. Randomly generated values let students to retry problems to obtain mastery. Teachers also receive detailed results that help them guide and monitor student progress.
Grades: 6–9
Cost: Free demo, subscription for students and families.

Learning Mathematics Successfully: Raising Self-Efficacy in Students, Teachers, and Parents
pp. 177–187
Copyright © 2019 by Information Age Publishing
177

Corbettmaths
https://corbettmaths.com
This resource from England provides math videos, math practice questions, and worksheets with answers.
Grades: K–12
Cost: Free

DragonBox
http://dragonbox.com
An award-winning series of math apps that harness the power of digital tools to create a better, deeper, more fun learning experience. Blogs, such as "Making Math Social" and "Saying No to Math Anxiety," are included as resources for teachers and parents.
Grades: K–6
Cost: Free trial; $

Dreambox
http://www.dreambox.com
An adaptive learning platform designed to complement classroom instruction and deliver results. Includes resources for teachers, student data reports, and instructive insights.
Grades: K–8
Cost: Free trial; $ subscription

Edgenuity
https://www.edgenuity.com
Online learning digital curriculum for primary or supplementary instruction. Give students the support they need exactly when they need it.
Grades: K–12
Cost: $

eMath Instruction
https://emathinstruction.com
This site provides e-textbooks, answer keys, video lessons, and printables for students and teachers of Algebra 1 and 2, geometry, and trigonometry.
Grades: 8–12
Cost: $

First in Math
https://www.firstinmath.com
We love the friendly competition and game-based content offered by First in Math. Kids gain skills practice and fluency as they play games targeted toward fact proficiency, automaticity, and logical thinking.
Grades: K–8
Cost: Free trial; $

Front Row (now called Freckle)
https://www.frontrowed.com
This website offers more than 30,000 math questions, starting with a diagnostic that assigns material at just the right level. Front Row also features lessons, assessments, and reports for teachers.
Grades: K–9
Cost: Free for teachers; $ for upgrades and other features

GregTangMath.com
http://gregtangmath.com
GregTangMath strives to provide unparalleled math lessons for students as well as professional development for in-service teachers. Games, puzzles, and other resources, like free downloads, worksheets/word problems, math centers.
Grades K–6
Cost: Free

Illuminations
https://illuminations.nctm.org
This site, from the National Council of Teachers of Mathematics, features complete lesson plans, mobile games for students, interactive activities, and brain teasers.
Grades: Pre-K–12
Cost: Free

Illustrative Math
https://www.illlustrativemathematics.org
High-quality educational resources for teachers and students. Excellent math tasks, videos, lesson plans, and problem-based curriculum modules.
Grades 6–8
Cost: Free

Istation
https://www.istation.com
Istation makes personalized learning easy with computer-adaptive instruction, assessments, personalized data profiles, and teacher resources. Includes digital lessons and face-to-face teaching strategies.
Grades: PreK–8
Cost: $

IXL Math
https://www.ixl.com/math/
This website offers real-world scenarios, and unlimited questions. Individualized math practice. Teachers can choose the strand and set up students to work independently.
Grades: K–12
Cost: $

Khan Academy
https://www.khanacademy.org
Khan Academy is a personalized learning resource available for all ages. Video learning segments are followed by practice activities.
Grades: K–12
Cost: Free

LearnZillion
https://learnzillion.com/p/
Cloud-based curriculum for K–12 students, focusing on supporting both traditional and blended classrooms.
Grades K–12
Cost: Free; $ premium version

Mathletics
http://us.mathletics.com
Online learning space that is engaging, supportive, and designed to increase interest in math while teaching state standards.
Grades: K–12
Cost: Free trial for teachers and families; $ subscription

MobyMax
http://www.mobymax.com
This program finds and fixes learning gaps with the power of personalized learning. Three-pronged approach features personalized learning, pinpoint assessments, and interactive classroom.
Grades: K–8

Cost: Free version includes all curriculum, one test per year, and basic overview of student progress; $ for personalized learning license

Origo Education
https://www.origoeducation.com
Stepping Stones, from Origo, is a unique and comprehensive curriculum that combines print and digital materials. It features problem-solving activities, strategies, and practice. Teachers also have access to a professional blog that provides advice and support.
Grades: K–6
Cost: $

PowerMyLearning
https://powermylearning.org/learn/academic-programs/schools/
This organization helps students in low-income communities, together with teachers and families, harness the power of digital learning platforms to raise educational outcomes. The program features school workshops, instructional coaching, and professional learning communities.
Grades: K–12
Cost: $

Prodigy Software
https://www.prodigygame.com
Math games tackle more than 1,200 crucial math skills in a fun and engaging way.
Grades: 1–8
Cost: Free for teachers; $ for family subscription

Skoolbo
https://skoolbo.com
Interactive, game-based learning world that motivates students through rewards. Features include daily challenge, step-by-step lessons, and parent connections.
Grades: K–5
Cost: Free; $ monthly fee

Splash Math
https://www.splashmath.com
Boost confidence, increase scores, and get ahead. Fun for enrichment or regular practice.
Grades K–5
Cost: Free basic plan; $ premium plan

SumDog
https://www.sumdog.com
Math games are engaging, evidence-based, adaptive learning. Focus on specific skills, target interventions, and make assessment easy.
Grades: K–5
Cost: Free trial; $ subscription

TenMarks
https://www.tenmarks.com/about
Award-winning online instructional program with rigorous content and curriculum resources for differentiated instruction and personalized learning.
Grades: K–12
Cost: Free 30 day trial; $ subscription

Woot Math
https://www.wootmath.com/practice
Woot Math offers adaptive practice for teaching rational numbers and related topics, such as fractions, decimals, and ratios.
Grades: 3–7
Cost: Free tier for teachers; additional features available for extra cost

Zearn
https://www.zearn.org
Personalized math curriculum that includes digital lessons and small-group instruction. Also has online modules, workbooks and answer keys, and professional development.
Grades: K–5
Cost: $

INTERACTIVE TOOLS TO USE IN INSTRUCTION

These sites offer engaging videos and tools to use in your daily math instruction.

BrainPOP
https://www.brainpop.com/math
Engaging animated learning videos, games, quizzes, and activities to encourage kids on their unique learning path.
Grades: preK–8
Cost: $

Desmos
https://www.desmos.com
An online graphing calculator that students can use for free. Includes a teacher-centric activity builder for creating digital math activities.
Grades: 9–12
Cost: Free

Flocabulary
https://www.flocabulary.com
Flocabulary offers songs, activities, and videos.
Grades K–12
Cost: Free trial; $ subscription

GeoGebra
https://www.Geogebra.org
Another graphing calculator for functions, geometry, algebra, calculus, statistics, and 3D math. Includes practice sheets.
Grades: 9–12
Cost: Free

Kahoot
https://kahoot.it
Kahoot is a game-based classroom response system played by the whole class in real time. Multiple-choice questions are projected on the screen, then students answer with their smartphone, tablet, or computer.
Grades K–12
Cost: Free 30-day trial; $ subscription

ACTIVITIES FOR INSTRUCTION AND INDEPENDENT PRACTICE

Arithmetic Four
http://www.shodor.org/interactivate/activities/ArithmeticFour/
Two users play a game in which each player tries to connect four game pieces in a row (like game Connect Four). The players answer math questions to connect the pieces. Teacher chooses how much time each player has to answer, the level of difficulty, and the type of math problem.
Grades: 2–8
Cost: Free

BeatCalc
http://mathforum.org/k12/mathtips/beatcalc.html
Just like it sounds, this game challenges students to beat a calculator. Features step-by-step directions for performing functions quickly.
Grades 3–8
Cost: Free

Coolmath Games
http://coolmath-games.com
This site offers hundreds of games.
Grades K–12
Cost: Free; $ ad-free version

Figure This!
http://figurethis.nctm.org
Figure This! is a site designed to encourage families to practice math together. It includes fun and engaging math games and high-quality challenges. It even offers challenges in Spanish.
Grades 6–8
Cost: Free

Free Rice
http://freerice.com/category
This math game serves a dual purpose. Students practice multiplication and prealgebra math. For each answer they get right, the World Food Programme donates 10 grains of rice to help end hunger.
Grades 3–7
Cost: Free

Jefferson Lab
https://education.jlab.org/indexpages/elementgames.html
Your students will love fun math games like Speed Math Deluxe, Mystery Math, Place Value Game, and more.
Grades 3–11
Cost: Free

MATHHelp.com
http://mathhelp.com
In-depth lessons with videos, guided practice, interactive self-tests, and more.
Grades: 5–12
Cost: Free

Math Playground
http:///www.mathplayground.com
More than 425 math games, logic puzzles, and brain workouts for students to practice their math skills.
Grades: 1–6
Cost: Free

MrNussbaumMath
http://mrnussbaum.com/math-for-kids
Nearly 100 original math games, workshops, and practice modules, as well as math printables.
Grades 1–6
Cost: Free

Ninja Maths
http://www.ninjamaths.com.au
This interactive, online tool helps students master basic facts. Set up as a whole-class or small-group competition, students earn ninja cards and track results on a ninja scoring poster. Two board games that teach operations are also available for purchase.
Grades 2–8
Cost: Free

Numeracy Ninjas
http://www.numeracyninjas.org
This is a free intervention tool designed to fill gaps in students' mental calculation skills and empower them with number fluency. Students can earn ninja belts of different colors for their skill level.
Grades 2–8
Cost: Free

PBS Math Club
https://www.pbslearningmedia.org/collection/pbs-math-club/#
.W1JGTrgnaUl
From PBS Learning Media, middle schoolers will learn from this video blog. Not only does each episode cover Common Core Standards, it makes math learning culturally relevant with pop-culture references.
Grades: 6–9
Cost: Free

Quizlet

https://quizlet.com
Students can create study flashcards, play learning games, practice skills, collaborate with other students, and more.
Grades: 5–12
Cost: Free

Reflex

https://www.reflexmath.com
Another resource to help students build fact fluency. Each game is tailored to students' ability levels.
Grades: 2–6
Cost: Free trial; $ monthly subscription

Sheppard Software

http://www.sheppardsoftware.com/math.htm
This site offers math games, from basic operations to algebra and geometry.
Grades: K–6
Cost: Free

That Quiz

https://www.thatquiz.org
Simple math test activities for teachers and students, from beginning math operations to calculus. Teachers set the skill level, number of problems, and time limit. A report, which tallies right and wrong answers, is provided after each quiz.
Grades 3–12
Cost: Free

Xtramath

https://xtramath.org/#/home/index
Xtramath is an interactive online tool that helps students practice and master basic arithmetic facts, it's quick and easy to use. Weekly emails provide progress reports for teachers and parents.
Grades: K–8
Cost: Free

TEACHER RESOURCES

The following are sources for teachers that provide lesson-planning resources and professional development materials.

Common Core Sheets
http://www.commoncoresheets.com
Math worksheets for just about any area of study. Free downloads. Good for planning lessons, review, and independent work.
Grades: K–6
Cost: Free

Mashup Math
http://mashupmath.com
Mashup Math has a library of 100+ math video-lessons as well as a You-Tube channel that features new math video-lessons every week. A free e-book of math challenges is also available.
Grades K–8
Cost: Free

Math-Aids
http://www.math-aids.com
Math worksheets for students, teachers and parents.
Grades: K–10
Cost: Free

MathsBot
http://mathsbot.com
Tools for math teachers, including bell-ringers and drills, math tools and manipulatives, question generators, printables, and puzzles.
Grades K–12
Cost: Free

National Library of Virtual Manipulatives (NLVM)
http://nlvm.usu.edu
This National Science Foundation-supported project provides a large library of uniquely interactive, web-based virtual manipulatives and concept tutorials for math instruction.
Grades: K–12
Cost: Free

TopMarks
http://www.topmarks.co.uk

ABOUT THE AUTHORS

Clark J. Hickman, EdD, is an associate research professor emeritus and associate dean emeritus of the College of Education at the University of Missouri-St. Louis. He earned his doctorate in educational psychology from the University of Missouri-St. Louis in 1993. His lifelong research interests have been the role of self-efficacy in changing teacher behaviors, whether it be through the adoption of new teaching methods, avoid burnout, or adapting to changes that increase student learning. Through his teaching of research methods and adolescent psychology courses, he witnessed firsthand the issues teachers face professionally in adapting to changes in education today and responded by developing grants, workshops, seminars, and conferences that addressed these issues. Dr. Hickman has published more than a dozen articles and book chapters on teacher professional development, educational technology, and teacher evaluation.

Helene J. Sherman, EdD, is an emeritus professor in the College of Education at the University of Missouri-St. Louis where she earned her doctorate degree in mathematics education. After teaching elementary school, middle school, and college mathematics, Dr. Sherman taught mathematics education courses while department chair and the associate dean for educator preparation in the college. Her research interests are the specific components in classroom mathematics instruction impacting student interest and achievement as well as translating best practices to teacher education curricula. Dr. Sherman has directed and codirected numerous statewide grant projects in K–12 school districts and is coauthor of digits, a middle grades math curriculum, published by Pearson Education, three K–8 metric measurement activity books and the textbook, *Teaching Learners Who Struggle With Mathematics: Responding With Systematic Intervention and Remediation* (4th ed.), published by Pearson Education and Waveland Press. She has published her work in numerous nationally peer-reviewed educational journals and is a frequent speaker at area and national conferences.

CPSIA information can be obtained
at www.ICGtesting.com
Printed in the USA
JSHW022030281019
2130JS00002B/14

9 781641 137379